ARTHUR AKUIEN CHOL

A LIFE
FIGHTING
FOR MY PEOPLE

ARTHUR AKUIEN CHOL

"Leadership is unlocking people's potential to become better" - Bill Bradley

Please be advised that this disclaimer serves to delineate the separation between the author's personal opinions and the viewpoint of Africa World Books, the publisher. The opinions articulated in this book belong solely to the author and may not necessarily harmonise with the publisher's perspective. Africa World Books releases this disclaimer to firmly establish that the author's viewpoints are distinct from the publisher's position. In any instance related to the author's personal opinions expressed within this book, the author shall be solely responsible and liable for them. Africa World Books explicitly disclaims any responsibility for the author's viewpoints, placing the onus for such opinions squarely on the author's shoulders.

The publisher wishes to acknowledge and thank Dr. Douglas H. Johnson for his invaluable help and support for Africa World Books and its mission of preserving and promoting African cultural and literary traditions and history. Dr. Johnson and fellow historians have been instrumental in ensuring that African people remain connected to their past and their identity. Africa World Books is proud to carry on this mission.

Copyright © 2023 Arthur Akuien Chol

ISBN (Paperback): 9780645759020
ISBN (eBook): 9780645759013

No part of this publication may be reproduced, stored in a retrieval system, or transmitted, in any form, or by any means, electronic, mechanical, photocopying, recording or otherwise, without the prior permission of the publishers.

This book is sold subject to the conditions that it shall not, by way of trade or otherwise, be lent, re-sold, hired out or otherwise circulated without the publisher's prior consent in any form of binding or cover other than in which it is published and without a similar condition including the condition being imposed on the subsequent purchaser.

Cover design, typesetting and layout: Africa World Books
Unit 3, 57 Frobisher St, Osborne Park, WA 6017
P.O. Box 1106 Osborne Park, WA 6916

TABLE OF CONTENTS

Prologue   7
A Snapshot of our History   8

Chapter 1: My Family   11
Chapter 2: My Childhood   17
Chapter 3: My Political Awakening   25
Chapter 4: Fighting for Independence   29
Chapter 5: Université Lovanium   37
Chapter 6: The University Of Freiburg   41
Chapter 7: Our Fight for Autonomy   47
Chapter 8: Bringing our People Home   53
Chapter 9: Becoming A Father   59

Chapter 10: Serving My People   63

Chapter 11: Minister for Commerce and Industry   69

Chapter 12: The Tragic Story of my Country   77

Chapter 13: Chairman Of Humanitarian Affairs   87

Chapter 14: A Fragile Peace   93

Chapter 15: South Sudan's First Minister of Finance   97

Chapter 16: Treachery   113

Chapter 17: Declaring My Innocence   119

Chapter 18: Achieving Independence   129

Chapter 19: Seeking Refuge in Australia   135

Epilogue   *139*

Acknowledgements   *143*

Photos   *147*

PROLOGUE

This is the story of my life, one that started as a traditional Dinka cattle boy in the remote grasslands of South Sudan and continues as a representative of my people in our country's political spectrum. To understand me and my journey, you need to understand the history of South Sudan because my life mirrors the struggle of my fellow countrymen for independence, peace and economic stability—the prerequisites for a harmonious society that offers its people the opportunity to break the cycle of poverty and build a future full of hope.

ARTHUR AKUIEN CHOL

A SNAPSHOT OF OUR HISTORY

After Sudan gained independence from Britain and Egypt in 1956, an elected Parliament ruled the country, and the seat of power was in Khartoum in the north of Sudan. The following year, a military regime overthrew the elected government and tried to force the people of South Sudan, who were Christian or followed tribal religions, to convert to Islam and embrace an Arab culture. That was the beginning of our struggle, with our initial objective being the call for a federal system of government.

My people in South Sudan wanted independence from the north so we could follow our own traditional norms, promote economic development, and build a strong, harmonious nation that served its people. But the country's rulers from the north disagreed.

What followed was decades of violent guerrilla warfare, two civil wars, and the death and displacement of millions of our people. In parallel, the country's rulers marginalised the people of South Sudan, starving the south of the funds it required to build a sustainable economy and provide infrastructure—basic services such as clean drinking water, electricity, sanitation, hospitals and schools.

In January 2011, after five decades of brutal conflict, the people of the Republic of South Sudan voted in a referendum to secede from Sudan. Six months later, in July 2011, South Sudan gained independence, becoming one of the world's newest nations. The people of the Republic of South Sudan as it became known, were ecstatic, and we had high hopes for peace, economic and social development, and stability.

Tragically, the foundations required to build strong political stability, economic sustainability and a peaceful society—governance, economic, judicial and security sector reform—were contested, and South Sudan descended into a violent civil war among its own people. What followed and continues today are human rights violations, internal displacement of our people, millions of refugees unable to return home, a hunger crisis, acute malnutrition of our children, and little hope of lifting the majority of our people out of extreme poverty.

Sadly, that is the tragic story of my country, providing the backdrop to my life story.

CHAPTER 1

MY FAMILY

I come from a long line of proud Dinka people. My family lived in a small village on ancestral land in Mangar Lual in Tiar Aliet Payam, Aweil South County, in Northern Bahr el Ghazal State-Aweil, 800 kilometres from Juba, South Sudan's capital. My waadit (grandfather), Dut Akol Angok, was born in 1850 and he raised cattle. His wife and my maadit, Akon Jieng, was born in 1870. At the turn of the twentieth century when she was 30, Maadit gave birth to my waa (father), Chol Dut Akol. My maa (mother), Achol Malong Majok was born in 1910.

When I arrived on 15 April 1942, I joined my two brothers, Angok Chol Dut, 12, and six-year-old Deng Chol Dut. Hospitals and health services were almost non-existent in our area because of a lack of investment by the national government in Sudan, so like my siblings and most children in the south of Sudan, I was born at home. Waa and Maa named me Akuien Chol and after being baptised, I became known as Arthur Akuien Chol because my family is Roman Catholic.

When I was two years old, Maa gave birth to my sister Awut Chol Dut. Five years later while giving birth to her fifth child, Maa died from blood loss. Without medical help, many women died during and immediately after childbirth, and infant immortality was high. Sadly, I do not remember much about Maa because I was only seven years old when she died. Waa and other relatives told me Maa was an impressive lady and highly respected. Kind and generous, she was popular, and many people came to our house to spend time with her, a typical communal way of living that has always been significant in our Dinka way of life.

The lack of basic infrastructure, such as hospitals, roads,

clean drinking water, electricity and schools, resulted from the nation's northern rulers marginalising the people of South Sudan. Dirt roads in my village were primitive, full of craters and turned to slippery mud during the wet season. Our village lacked clean drinking water, so multiple times each day the women had to trudge to the well carrying empty 18-litre jerry cans. At the well, they queued for hours in the scorching sun or torrential rain for their turn to fill the container. Once full, the cans weighed 19 kilograms, and the women walked home balancing them on their heads. Being forced to spend so much time fetching water held women back from paid work and young girls missed out on school because they had to collect water for their families.

Our houses lacked electricity, so we used firewood for light and the women cooked on open charcoal fires. They had to walk into the forest to collect firewood and as they cut more and more trees, their journey became longer. Once again, rather than sending their children to school to receive the education they needed to break the poverty cycle, parents kept young girls at home so they could fetch water, collect firewood and do household chores. And young boys missed out on school because they had to look after their family's cattle and goats.

Lack of investment in education by the northern power elites meant the south had few government schools. Missionaries ran schools in some villages, but the standard of education was poor because the missionaries were not qualified teachers. The few children from rural villages who went to a government school had to leave home and live in dormitories a long way from their villages. That was my experience, but more about that later.

The challenges almost every child endured to gain an education were enormous; I was one of those children. Rates of illiteracy when I was a child were far too high and remain so, trapping my people in poverty from one generation to the next. To lift our people out of poverty, we must provide boys and girls with quality education. But first, we must provide clean drinking water and electricity to free them from the daily chores that keep them away from school.

It is still far too difficult and expensive to put a child through primary school in South Sudan, but I believe it can be done if our leaders put their energies into it. The quality of education in South Sudan might never achieve global standards, but we must give parents the opportunity to offer their children the best start in life by providing good schools, textbooks and professionally qualified teachers. The country has however, managed to oversee some of its educational institutions being empowered, and I am personally delighted to witness the transformation of Juba university among others, to the high standard it has achieved.

CHAPTER 2

MY CHILDHOOD

After Maa died, Waa took care of us, bringing all the things we needed into our house. Affectionate and easy-going, he loved children. I remember him fondly. Waa was an active member of the Dinka community and popular among our people. I mostly remember him for always prioritising the welfare of his family; he was my role model. Waa herded cattle at riverside camps in the dry season and grew millet, sorghum, fruit and vegetables during the rainy season. We ate what Waa grew, and he exchanged what we did not need for basics such as sugar, salt and cooking oil.

My family lived in a traditional African mud house with a thatched grass roof. The roof was sloped and conical. It was also high to allow heat to rise and flow out through the top. We had four huts: one for Waa and Maa when she was still alive, another for the children and Maadit who lived with us, one for cooking, and another that acted as a rudimentary bathroom.

Our house did not have electricity, so we used firewood for lighting. It was pitch black at night and the stars twinkled brightly because our village was in a rural area, far from city lights. After sunset, life ground to a halt in the village and it was silent; all I could hear were the crickets and mosquitoes. Wild animals roamed our village, so we had to keep an eye out for them when we went outside at night.

Our village lacked clean running water so Maadit and later, Awut my sister, had to walk along dirt roads to a well to fetch water. Navigating the boggy roads during the rains was almost impossible and took much longer than in the dry season. Multiple trips a day to the well were necessary to get enough water for drinking, cooking, bathing and washing the clothes. Our house did not have a toilet, so we would dig a hole in the ground or find a tree. As we chopped more and more trees down for firewood, the walk to find a tree became longer, which was dangerous for Maadit and Awut at night.

Maadit cooked outside in the courtyard on a tin grill called a *kanoon*, using charcoal she had burned down from wood. We did not have a fridge, so she would cook fresh food for our family every day. My favourite foods were *asida*, a lump of dough, and *kisra*, a flat bread, both made from millet. We ate raw vegetables, or a vegetable stew. A staple dish was dry fish and dry meat, which we often ate with *asida* or *kisra*. To make tea, Maadit would rely on tea leaves that Waa brought home from exchanges with traders who would visit our area from time to time.

From the age of five, I looked after Waa's goats and sheep and Angok and Deng supervised Waa's cattle. During the dry season once I was older, I joined Waa and my brothers in cattle camps in the *toic*, areas close to rivers that flood during the wet season. Once the rains stopped, the *toic* was covered in lush grass so our cattle could graze there for several months. As traditional Dinka cattle boys living in cattle camps, we covered our bodies in cow dung and ash from the campfires instead of wearing clothes, something that would later get me into trouble. At night, we used woven mats to cover ourselves if it rained. Every day in the camp, we would milk the cows and drink the milk as our principal source of food.

When the rain arrived each June, we would return to our village, and the cattle lived outside or in *Luak*, thatched grass and mud huts built for cattle, goats and sheep. During the wet season, Waa would grow millet, sorghum and vegetables. The day started at dawn when the roosters woke us up and from then on Angok, Deng and I would do chores such as cleaning the *Luak*, throwing away the cow dung or drying it to keep insects and mosquitoes away. Sometimes I would milk the goats and sheep and my brothers would milk the cows.

When I was eight, Waa decided I should go to school. Abuok Deng Gai, who was from my village and would later become my brother-in-law, also encouraged me to go to school because he was already a student and among the first from my village to attain a formal education. The closest government school was 50 kilometres away, so to study I would have to leave home and live in a dormitory with other kids from around South Sudan. But Maadit disagreed with Waa. I guess she did not understand British policies in Sudan back then.

'Akuien an orphan,' Maadit pleaded. 'He should remain at home with us.'

Waa looked across at me. 'What do you want to do?' he asked.

'I want to go to school,' I said.

'Then it's settled, you'll go to school,' he smiled.

At the beginning of the first term, I set off on foot with my friend Celestino Mawien Kuc and other boys from the area; we walked 50 kilometres to Mathiang Elementary School, a newly opened government school in Northern Bahr el Ghazal State-Aweil. My classmates and I lived together in a dormitory and the government provided us with bedding, books, uniforms and food, although Waa gave me a milking cow to provide extra nourishment. It was a common practice for parents to send their child to school with their own milking cow.

During my first year, I ran into trouble with the headmaster one weekend after I joined a group of classmates at a cattle camp. It seemed like such a natural thing to do after my upbringing as a Dinka cattle boy. We left school wearing our clothes but took them off when we arrived at the cattle camp. That was our first mistake. The second was we decorated our naked bodies with ashes and cow manure, although we did not know it was a mistake.

On our way back to the school dormitory, we ran into the headmaster, Mr Philbeto. I cannot remember his second name, but he was from the fartit tribe of Western Bahr el Ghazal-Wau. He scowled as he approached us. 'Why are you naked and covered in ash?' he roared, glaring at us with angry eyes. As I now recall, we were young then and did not really understand the value of education.

'It's our traditional culture,' I explained. 'We wanted to enjoy our time at the cattle camp.'

Mr Philbeto ordered us to see him the next day, a Monday. At the morning assembly, he ordered me and my friends to come forward and stand on a raised platform. In a derogatory tone, he told everyone we had visited a cattle camp on the weekend, stripped naked, then covered our naked bodies with ashes and cow dung. After humiliating us in front of our classmates and teachers, he lashed each of us with a cane 10 times. It hurt, and of course, we screamed in pain, a second humiliation.

This punishment infuriated one of the bigger boys so much he ran into the woodlands, returning with a big stick he used to lash Mr Philbeto. Some bigger boys rescued the headmaster, and, between them, they restrained the attacker. After detaining him, Mr Philbeto handed him over to the district police commissioner, a colonial administrator—Sudan was still under British control in 1950. The commissioner was furious when he noticed the boy's hands were tied, ordering Mr Philbeto to untie them and set the boy free to return to school.

During the colonial period, our people did not like their children leaving home to live in dormitories at school, and Mr Philbeto's harsh punishment risked angering parents. The British administrator knew the headmaster's behaviour might have prompted parents to remove their children from school, a calamity for South Sudan, because so few children went to school. To prevent this, he called all the chiefs, assuring them it would never happen again. That act by the British commissioner saved me and other children from being taken out of school, the first ever to be established in my community.

Once each year, I travelled home to visit my family for a 15-day holiday. On my first trip back home, Waa welcomed me by slaughtering a goat and cooking it on the charcoal. I was happy to be with my family after so long away from them, but heartbroken to learn Maadit had died while I was away.

At the end of the holidays, Angok and Deng said I should remain at home to help them look after Waa's cattle.

'No!' Waa insisted. 'Akuien is going back to school.'

I longed to return to school because I had made several friends and learned to read and write. Angok and Deng were not happy with Waa's decision, but they had to obey him. After my holiday, Waa took me back to Northern Bahr el Ghazal State-Aweil, and I started my second year at Mathiang Elementary School.

In 1954, I finished elementary school and returned home. My milking cow was 'retired', and I took her home with me. Waa slaughtered a bull to welcome me, and he hosted a big celebration for our relatives and friends. Everyone was happy for me, especially my brothers, because they could see how far I'd advanced in my education. By then, Angok was married and occupied with his wife and children, and Deng was busy planning his wedding.

Waa wanted me to continue my education and so did I. At the end of that holiday, Waa gave me some pocket money and I packed my school bag ready to travel on a government bus to Tonj Intermediate School, over 200 kilometres away.

CHAPTER 3

MY POLITICAL AWAKENING

In the lead up to Sudan gaining independence from the British and Egyptians, the British favoured the north and appointed only three people from the south to senior positions in the future government of Sudan. That is where our problems started, when our people discovered South Sudan was left out of the nation's governing body. The north also dominated Sudan's army and other security sectors.

Naturally, my people grew increasingly frustrated and angry. They proposed a federal system of government, but leaders from the north disagreed. In protest, soldiers from South Sudan rebelled, orchestrating a mutiny in Torit on 18 August 1955, four months before Sudan gained independence from British and Egyptian rule. It was our people's first known struggle for independence.

The Torit mutiny took place three months into my school year at Tonj. My teachers told us about the mutiny and what caused it; it was my political awakening. At 13, I became enlightened about the political desperation of my people and resolved to fight for their rights. I realised we might even need to form our own country.

Shortly after the mutiny, which occurred 700 kilometres from Tonj, schools across the south were forced to close and reluctantly, I returned to Aweil. Once home, I spent my days with Waa, Angok and Deng at the cattle camp. I also hunted with my friends and enjoyed a simple village life. Still, I loved learning and advancing in school and found the transition back to life in a cattle camp difficult. Leaving school because of war and insecurity disappointed me, but I had no choice; it caused much uncertainty in my mind.

It took the national authorities a year to quell the

anti-government mutiny, and once it did, schools reopened in the south of Sudan. The authorities advised the district commissioner to inform all the chiefs to gather the students and transport them back to their schools. It made me happy to know I was returning to school, and I prepared myself for the journey to Tonj in a bus provided by the government.

On 1 January 1956 when I was 14, Sudan gained independence from Britain and Egypt. The government of Sudan was formed and Khartoum, in the north, became the seat of power. However, the Prime Minister, Ismail al-Azhari, declared his intention to make Sudan an Islamic republic. Most people in the north followed Islam, but in the south Italian Catholic missionaries and Anglicans had established churches and schools during colonial rule and the people of South Sudan were predominantly Christian; they feared Islam because of its bitter history of slavery, economic exploitation, uneven economic opportunity and political isolation.

Two years after Sudan gained independence, the military overthrew the government in a bloodless coup and military chief General Ibrahim Abboud became the President (1958-1964). Consistent with its policy of 'Sudanisation', the military government made Sunday a working day in the south and Friday—the Muslim holy day—a resting day. This provoked Southerners and students from all over the south, including me, to go on strike. We also organised demonstrations against the military regime. Although the north banned them, demonstrations and rallies by students and urban elites occurred across the nation.

The government's new policies prompted several senior students to leave Sudan and seek political asylum in east African nations. Some politicians from the south—William Deng Nhial, Joseph Oduho, Father Setrino and Marko Rome—also fled the country when the military rulers dissolved the Parliament and banned all political activity. William Deng Nhial led the protest movement in Khartoum, but once political activity was banned, he sought asylum in Kenya with the support of a charity organisation.

Meanwhile, I graduated from Tonj Intermediate School and enjoyed a holiday at home with my family. Afterwards, I travelled 370 kilometres by bus to Rumbek Secondary School in Rumbek, the capital of Lakes State in central South Sudan. It was 1959 and I was 17 years old. At the time, I did not realise many of our nation's future leaders were my classmates or schoolmates.

CHAPTER 4

FIGHTING FOR INDEPENDENCE

In 1962, a group of exiled politicians formed the Sudan African National Union (SANU) to fight for the independence of South Sudan, unanimously electing William Deng as the leader. Deng started mobilising students and politicians from the south to join them, and the exiled South Sudanese politicians such as Dominic Muorwel and Wek Athian joined him. Around this time, we heard exiles from the south had bought arms from the military base, Bunyia, in the Congo, then secretly carried them into the south of Sudan. They planned to begin a guerrilla war to gain South Sudan's independence from the north.

That was the beginning of Sudan's first civil war, which was led by the southern separatist Anya Nya movement. Towns and villages were destroyed, houses and crops burned, and livestock killed or stolen. Many people died of starvation and disease. Families were separated and thousands of children who fled on their own were recruited as soldiers.

When the civil war started, I was in my third year at Rumbek Secondary School. The following year, my fellow students and I heard exiled politicians in Congo and east Africa had amassed plenty of arms, and they needed students to join the rebellion and liberate Southern Sudan. This was the time I knew I had to fight for our people. Our thinking was to first liberate southern Sudan from the Arabs and Islamic system, then we could return to complete our education. We thought it would take two years. How wrong we were.

In 1963 at 21, I finished the Cambridge certificate, attaining first grade marks. The University of Khartoum offered me a place to study law, but I opted to follow our leader, William Deng Nhial, and join the liberation struggle. On 19 June 1963, I left school with 10 of my classmates to join the political agitation movement.

That was the start of a 12-day trek through the forest from Wau in north-west Sudan down to Obo in the Central African Republic to meet up with William Deng. My family did not know where I was. The oldest among us was Kawach Makuei, who was in his 30s and married; he left his wife and children in South Sudan to join us in our trip to OBO, Central Africa. Kawach was worldly-wise and gave us quick lessons on how to use the position of the sun to guide us and tell us the time.

When we left Wau, we carried a few clothes and some food, but our food supplies ran out after a few days. From then on, we foraged for wild honey and fruit, leaving us ravenous. No-one thought to take weapons to protect ourselves, which was a big mistake because it meant we could not hunt wild animals for food. Luckily, there was plenty of water in the creeks and rivers for us to drink. To get across rivers, we dragged fallen trees and abandoned logs onto the riverbanks, using them as boats.

Something else we did not think to take with us was a compass, or even a map, so day after day we trekked through the bush along the tracks of wild animals, using the position of the sun to guide us. At sunset, we would light a fire, then sit around eating whatever food we had foraged. At night, we slept on pieces of bark, taking it in turns to stay awake and guard the group.

The area was full of wild elephants, buffalos and other wild animals, but they were not used to seeing humans, so they would run away. On the third day, we chanced on a buffalo giving birth and she charged on us, almost killing one of my friends. Luckily, we all escaped, but it was a close call.

On the thirteenth day of our trek, we found a farmer who took us to Obo, a remote town in the south-eastern corner of the Central African Republic. It is so inaccessible, it is known as one of the toughest places on the continent to reach. By that stage, we'd walked 415 kilometres. In Obo, we spent two days resting and preparing for our journey to the Congo.

While in Obo, we met some refugees from Zandeland in southern Sudan. They told us there were many South Sudanese refugees in Paulis, a town in the Democratic Republic of Congo. The next day, we left, the start of a 700-kilometre trek to Paulis.

What followed was days and days of trekking through the forest. It was a great relief when we finally reached

Paulis and found the refugee camp; for the first time, we felt safe. US Aid provided us with plenty of food and fresh clothes, some of which we sold to give us much-needed cash. US Aid also erected tents, so we slept in them or in local houses. During our time in the camp, we lived well.

At the refugee camp, we met Wek Athian and Elia Duang Arop, both exiled politicians and some senior secondary school students, Angelo Beda and Phillip Mguee. They were trying to work out how to mobilise the refugees and connect them with William Deng. They told us Deng was coming to meet us in the camp to organise military training.

A week after we arrived in Paulis, William Deng turned up and met everyone in the camp. He asked us about the situation in South Sudan because we were the most recent arrivals.

'Our people are so frightened by the harsh new system and being forced to accept Islam, they are fleeing the country in large numbers,' we explained.

William Deng nodded and furrowed his brow. A look of intense sadness but also anger flashed across his face.

'Our people are ready to fight the military rulers,' I said. 'We just need weapons and training.'

When William Deng noticed most of us were students,

he urged us to complete our education before joining the Sudan African National Union.

'This war is going to take a long time,' he said. 'It's better you all go to study and leave us here to fight.'

'No, we want to fight for our country,' we protested.

'It's vital for South Sudan's future you study and become doctors, lawyers and politicians, our future leaders, so you can help our people,' he said.

'No, we want to fight,' we pleaded.

'If you join the fight on the ground now, you risk missing out on the education you need to lead the fight at a political level and liberate our country,' Deng insisted, assuring us he would help us get into a university in the Congo. 'You can join me once you graduate.'

At the refugee camp, I was reunited with Reverend Salvatore Atak Riak, a South Sudanese Catholic priest and one of Waa's relatives. In Sudan, Reverend Atak and I had met regularly and during my years at school, we'd stayed in touch. A politically minded person, he'd studied in Germany, then returned to Sudan to support South Sudanese political activities. But in 1964, he had to flee the country and seek refuge in the Democratic Republic of Congo because his life was in danger after the Sudanese regime expelled Catholic missionaries from South Sudan.

William Deng spoke with a couple of charities in Khartoum, and they smuggled our high school certificates to the Congo without the knowledge of the Sudanese government. Deng then helped us apply to study at universities in the Congo, West Africa and Europe.

Meanwhile, Deng and his followers recruited high school graduates from the south who did not qualify to study at university, gave them weapons and trained them inside South Sudan, near the border with the Congo. The Sudan African National Union's first attack on the government took place in 1964 in Wau. South Sudanese police and prisoners joined the fight, but sadly, our forces were defeated. The government captured many of our soldiers and imprisoned them, sentencing some to death. Undeterred, our people raised funds for William Deng to purchase arms and continue our people's fight for independence.

To my delight, Université Lovanium in the Belgium Congo offered me a place to study French. A Catholic Jesuit university, it was near Kinshasa, the capital of the Democratic Republic of the Congo. To fund my studies, Reverend Atak organised a scholarship for me through the Catholic church and Jesuit charities. The scholarship covered all my expenses at university, and I even had a small amount of pocket money. I felt like I was on my way to gaining the education I needed.

CHAPTER 5

UNIVERSITÉ LOVANIUM

When I first arrived at the Université Lovanium and chatted with some teachers and students, I learned it was considered the best university in Africa. Well-funded, it received subsidies from the colonial government, two American foundations and the US Agency for International Development in Sudan. I enjoyed studying and was conscientious, but also closely followed political developments in the Sudan. After a few weeks, I joined a group of students, and we planned a series of political activities. Many of the students were from the Congo and they told us about the Republic of the Congo's political upheaval and conflict, which mirrored our own. To an extent, this was also a platform where I'd also echo my people's woes.

We learned that as soon as the Republic of the Congo gained independence from Belgium in 1960, conflict erupted, leading to a series of civil wars. Congo's leaders asked the United Nations for help to defuse what was known as the Congo Crisis. At the time, Dag Hammarskjöld, a Swedish economist and diplomat, was Secretary-General of the United Nations, and he sent 20,000 peacekeepers to the Congo. He also made four trips there while trying to negotiate ceasefire agreements. Tragically, on 18 September 1961, when Hammarskjöld was en route to continue these negotiations, his plane crashed, and he perished, along with seven other United Nations staff members and the Swedish crew. It was a stark reminder to us of the perils of fighting for independence.

Meanwhile, I completed my French course at the Université Lovanium. I planned to remain there to study medicine, but to my dismay learned it was a five-year course, and I could only get a scholarship for four years. Fortunately, I received an offer to study economics at The University of Freiburg in 1967, a Jesuit university in Switzerland. I happily accepted this opportunity. Reverend Atak connected me with the Jesuit Social Service, a charity organisation in Switzerland, and it offered me a scholarship.

Several senior students from Rumbek Secondary School in South Sudan were already in Freiburg University, including Lawrence Wol Wol, a leader who was representing the South Sudanese students in Europe. Moung Akot, Leah Merloke, Richard Okel and George Moras also studied there. I resolved to join them in our people's fight for independence.

CHAPTER 6

THE UNIVERSITY OF FREIBURG

In 1967 after Freiburg University offered me a place to study economics and Reverend Salvatore Atak Riak secured a scholarship for me, he gave me a one-way plane ticket for me to fly from Kinshasa in the Congo to Geneva. That was my first time in an aeroplane, an extraordinary experience. It was fascinating and also exhilarating to see villages, mountains, lakes, the ocean and cities through the window of the plane. Once the plane landed in Geneva, I asked some fellow passengers for directions, and they told me which train to catch to Freiburg, which was 140 kilometres away from the airport. I set off on my own, despite everything being new to me, including Switzerland's highly advanced rail system. When I reached The University of Freiburg, a student took me to the office of Reverend Foyer St Jostine, the priest in charge of students.

After chatting for a while, Reverend St Jostine escorted me to my room, which was ready for me. I rested then walked to the restaurant Reverend St Jostine had suggested. As I stepped inside, I felt overwhelmed to see students of so many nationalities. It was the first time I'd met people from Asia, Iran and West Africa. Many of the students introduced themselves and asked where I was from. We enjoyed a good meal together, then I returned to my room to sleep and prepare for my first day studying economics.

The following morning, I met Reverend Bernard Dean Wild, and he briefed me about the university and my scholarship. He told me my school fees were fully paid and my accommodation guaranteed, adding that the scholarship included 20 francs each month as pocket money. The Freiburg University campus was in the centre of the town and a short walk away from my accommodation, so Reverend Wild accompanied me. When we reached the lecture theatre, he introduced me to my classmates, many of whom came from Rwanda, the Congo and Nigeria.

As I sat in my first lecture, I felt tremendously happy. All the lectures were in French, a relief because after two years studying the language at Université Lovanium, I spoke it fluently and still do over 50 years later. I felt comfortable with my lectures, classmates and teachers. After I settled into university life, I started contacting my relatives in Sudan. While communication technologies were not as advanced as today, I often corresponded through writing letters to my only contact person, my good friend Clestino Mawien Kuc, who was studying at the University of Khartoum. Having spent our childhood and early school years together, he was a trustworthy friend who would also inform my family about my wellbeing and how I was proceeding with my studies abroad.

Shortly after arriving in Freiburg, I asked Reverend Atak, who was still in the Congo, to assist my friend Elijah Malok Aleng with a scholarship to join me at the university. Elijah was still in a refugee camp in Kinshasa in the Congo. Reverend Atak agreed and secured a four-year scholarship for Elijah to study economics as well.

The following year when Elijah arrived, I was incredibly happy, and remember helping him to settle into his accommodation in the same compound as mine. During university holidays, Elijah and I worked as labourers in factories to support ourselves financially.

Elijah and I began our political activities in Freiburg by contacting Lawrence Wol Wol. By this time, our fellow countrymen were scattered all over the world, so Lawrence, Elijah and my Sudanese friends Moung Akot, Leah, Richard, George Moras and I explored options for organising them politically, especially those in Europe. We also wanted to work out how to meet with politicians in Switzerland, France and Israel because those nations supported the South Sudanese cause and our struggle for independence.

In 1970, Lawrence Wol Wol invited me to travel to Israel to represent South Sudan at an international student union meeting. He wanted me to present our case for the liberation of South Sudan. Israel supported our military leader, Joseph Lagu, who collaborated with Gordon Mortat in the military wing, but we needed it to provide more political, military and financial assistance. During the event, I felt I did not disappoint. My participation was subjective considering my experiences and those of my people back at home in Sudan.

Once back in Freiburg, I connected with my friends and some Nigerian students from Biafra. They were from the Igbo ethnic group, a predominantly Christian group in the State of Biafra and they were fighting for the independence of Biafra from the Muslim-led military government of Nigeria. Their leader, Chukwuemeka 'Emeka' Odumegwu-Ojukwu, had formed a breakaway political party to fight for independence and it was active in Europe, particularly France. Whenever Ojukwu's supporters travelled to Europe throughout the Nigerian Civil War, we met with them.

Tragically, in 1970, Ojukwu and his troops were defeated by the Nigerian Government, which was supported by Britain and Russia. On the eve of Biafra's surrender, Ojukwu fled to Côte d'Ivoire on the coast of west Africa, where he was granted asylum. His defeat strengthened their resolve to continue with the guerrilla war.

Meanwhile, on 25 May 1969, Colonel Jaafar Muhammad an-Nimeiry led a coup d'état in Khartoum, removing President Ismail al-Azhari and his government. The coup signalled the end of Sudan's second democratic era because Nimeiry established a one-party state. The Sudanese Socialist Union was the sole legal political entity in the country and Nimeiry pursued socialist and

Pan-Arabist policies. Nimeiry's government pushed for an end to the First Sudanese Civil War, which by then had continued for nearly 14 years. In pursuing peace, the new government pushed for amnesty, and two weeks later, declared regional autonomy for South Sudan.

At the end of 1971, I graduated with a Bachelor of Economics degree from The University of Freiburg. An insurance company in Switzerland, Bahl, offered me a job, so I stayed there to make some money before returning to South Sudan to be part of our country's development and support my country's struggle for independence.

CHAPTER 7

OUR FIGHT FOR AUTONOMY

After he became Sudan's President, Colonel Nimeiry learned how badly Southerners had been marginalised since Sudan gained independence from the United Kingdom and Egypt in 1956. He wanted to unite the country and end the civil war, which was costly for his government and the people of Sudan. Joseph Lagu and Anyanya, the southern Sudanese separatist rebel army, led the civil war. Lagu, a politician and military leader from South

Sudan, was fighting for South Sudan's independence and self-determination and Nimeiry knew to end the war, his government would need to grant South Sudan autonomy.

In 1971, to bring an end to the civil war, Nimeiry started a series of talks with the Southern Sudan Liberation Movement. The All-Africa Conference of Churches and World Council of Churches mediated these talks. A year later, in May 1972, Nimeiry invited leaders from the Southern Sudan Liberation Movement to negotiate a peace agreement in Addis Ababa in Ethiopia. The Emperor of Ethiopia Hai el salasi and the All-Africa Conference of Churches mediated the negotiations. But some groups in South Sudan who were fighting the regime refused to take part in the talks: Gordon Mortart, who was a leader of another political party and Mayar Akoon, who was in the Congo.

Abel Alier Kwai, a Dinka, South Sudanese politician and Sudan's Vice-President, was a key negotiator in the peace talks. As well as being a politician, Abel was a judge, human rights lawyer and had studied at Rumbek High School, although a decade earlier than me. He was also an activist on behalf of Christians in Sudan. Abel was the leader of South Sudan inside the government and all those in exile, and he urged representatives of different groups to come to the table to negotiate a lasting solution to political differences. Abel led the delegation representing the Government of Sudan, and Ezboni Mondiri, a politician from South Sudan, led the delegation of the Southern Sudan Liberation Movement. Mondiri advocated for an equal federation of northern and southern states, with English and Arabic given equal recognition. He also proposed a secular state, with Islam and Christianity recognised as the two major religions, but each would be respected. Mondiri argued that the south should have a separate civil service, educational system and army.

During the peace negotiations, Abel and other politicians in South Sudan contacted me and my friends in Switzerland. At one stage, Abel visited us in Switzerland to discuss our position and seek our support for the negotiations. The peace talks were successful and opposing parties signed The Addis Ababa Agreement, a set of compromises within a treaty that granted South Sudan independence through a separate legislative and executive body.

The Addis Ababa Agreement granted regional autonomy to Southern Sudan, enabling it to develop its own democratic institutions. It also meant South Sudan would no longer be divided into the three separate regions

Al-Istiwā'iyyah (Equatoria), Baḥr al-Ghazāl, and Aʿālī al-Nīl (Upper Nile), and the soldiers of Anyanya would be integrated into the Sudanese army and police force.

Th Agreement was included in the Regional Self-Government Act of March 1972, and it was integrated into the permanent constitution of 1973. It meant the South gained an autonomous regional government with executive and legislative powers within a united Sudan. The South was also able to elect and remove the President of the High Executive Council. It could vote to request exemptions from any national legislation considered destructive to regional interests and allowed to raise revenues from local taxation; Khartoum agreed to provide additional revenues. However, Khartoum would continue to control economic planning and education.

Abel was instrumental in negotiating The Addis Ababa Agreement, ending the 17-year-long civil war. Afterwards, our people agreed Abel would lead the South Sudan government, and they appointed him as President of the High Executive Council of the Southern Sudan Autonomous Region. Joseph Lagu remained as head of the army, but he was disgruntled, because Abel was appointed to the role Lagu coveted. It would have grave consequences for future peace in the South.

A priority project after The Addis Ababa Agreement was signed was bringing Sudanese refugees home from neighbouring countries. Nemeiry accepted it would be costly, but fortunately, United Nations relief bodies offered to help. It would be one of the biggest repatriation programs ever undertaken by the High Commission for Refugees (UNHCR), aided by humanitarian non-governmental organisations such as the African Committee for the Relief of the Southern Sudanese, Norwegian Church AID, Oxfam, World Service, the Catholic Organization, the Catholic Charity Caritas and the Red Cross. At the time, they did not know they would remain active in Southern Sudan for 25 five years. I also did not know I would play a vital role in this effort.

CHAPTER 8

BRINGING OUR PEOPLE HOME

In 1972 after The Addis Ababa Agreement was signed and the Government of South Sudan was being formed, Lawrence Wol Wol introduced me to Clement Mboro, a Southern politician. Our political activities as South Sudanese university students in Switzerland and other activities across Europe were highly visible. In the same year, I would be called back from Switzerland to serve on the Commission for Resettlement. The commission was a committee of seven government employees who repatriated South Sudanese people who'd fled their homes during the civil war. The refugees lived in neighbouring countries such as the Congo, Central Africa, Uganda, Kenya and Ethiopia.

The first thing I did when I returned to Sudan was visit Waa and my brothers and sister. By then I'd been away from Sudan for 10 years and my family thought I was dead because I had not communicated with them. Waa slaughtered a bull, and all my relatives joined us to celebrate my safe return. I was one of the first Dinka in the region to graduate from university, so my family was incredibly proud of me. My homecoming event shaped and encouraged me to keep thriving for my people's sake. I still remember the joy and emotions my people showed, which, in turn, was a way of appreciating my achievements.

The head of the Commission for Resettlement, Clement Mboro, could not speak French, so whenever he travelled to the Congo, Central African Republic or other French-speaking countries, I accompanied him, serving as his interpreter. Our first trip was to neighbouring countries to assess the number of refugees we needed to repatriate to South Sudan. It astonished us to discover it was around 60,000.

Once Clement and I returned to South Sudan, we submitted a report to the government detailing the magnitude of the resettlement effort. Shortly afterwards, the government provided funds and our committee, led by Clement Mboro, commissioned traders to travel to neighbouring countries to bring the refugees home to South Sudan. International organisations such as the United Nations supported us and so did the governments of the Congo, Central Africa, Uganda, Kenya and Ethiopia.

The first refugees we returned were living in camps in the Congo. At first, they stayed in camps in Eastern and Western Equatoria, then they were taken to their ancestral lands and villages. The government provided them with food, medical supplies and money to re-build their houses and farms destroyed during the war. Once refugees living in camps in the Congo were resettled, we repatriated refugees from Uganda then Ethiopia, Kenya and Central Africa.

At first, I lived in Khartoum with other members of the Commission for Resettlement, but once the Government of South Sudan was formed, we all lived in Juba, the capital of South Sudan. My friend Elijah Malok Aleng, who studied with me at Rumbek Senior Secondary School and Freiburg University, returned to Sudan a year after me and we shared a flat in Juba town. The building belonged to Abdilfadil Agot, who was among the most successful Southern traders at the time.

During the next two years, we repatriated 40,000 refugees. I also helped some of my colleagues return from exile. Included were Dr Patric Nicola and my close friend Dr Atem Adual, who had both studied medicine in the Congo. Afterwards, I supported them in joining the Ministry of Health in Sudan. Another colleague I helped return, Angelo Beda, was studying in Lagos, Nigeria. Ajou Akuey Ajou was the only exile who refused to return from the Congo because he did not want to come back to an Arab country.

The 10 years following the agreement would give Sudan the longest period of relative peace in its history, although conflict bubbled under the surface because the agreement did not dispel the tensions that had originally caused the civil war. Tragically, the north's economic and political marginalisation of the south continued, leading to increased conflict and civil unrest in the south throughout the 1970s and beyond.

In 1974 I was appointed as chairman of the Regional Development Corporation, which was set up to boost economic growth, improve social infrastructure and provide basic services such as clean drinking water, electricity, schools and health services to improve the living conditions of our people. The corporation also aimed to strengthen governance and security and create new industries to provide employment opportunities. I organised branches of the corporation in Juba, Malakal and Wau and employed experienced directors, deputy directors and many other employees. Several corporations created during the colonial period were brought under my responsibility, including the Anzara sugar project in the Equatoria Region and the Simsim project in Yirol.

One of the corporation's roles was transporting essential commodities from Khartoum to South Sudan. Food was moved from Khartoum to Wau by rail, and steamers carried food to Juba. We also brought various items from neighbouring countries in East Africa to Juba and building materials from the north of Sudan.

However, Khartoum kept interfering with Abel Alier Kwai's programs, stalling progress on crucial Southern infrastructure and economic development projects. These projects had immense potential for boosting economic and social development, but it could not be realised because of the north's continued interference. Apart from the north's meddling, other reasons for disappointing results were a lack of logical planning and supervision by the southern regional government and insufficient coordination of the projects of various agencies. Several coffee, tea and forestry initiatives were progressed, and several road and rural water projects were spearheaded, especially in Equatoria, but in the end, development was uneven. The least developed areas were Bahr al Ghazal and Upper Nile.

The lack of economic and infrastructure development in the South disappointed and saddened me deeply, so at the end of 1974, I stood for election in the Parliament of Sudan. I believed I could put my education to the best use by representing my people and giving them a voice at a national level.

But first I had to attend to family matters.

CHAPTER 9

BECOMING A FATHER

When I returned to South Sudan, I asked Waa to find a wife for me because arranged marriages are the custom in Sudan. In 1974 at the age of 32, I became engaged to a Muslim Dinka girl from Bor, but her father was a dedicated South Sudanese Muslim, and he insisted I convert to Islam. As a Christian, I could not do that, so I ended the engagement. Afterwards, I returned home, and Waa arranged for me to marry Teresa Awien Mawien Diing, a

Catholic girl and from my village. Teresa and I married in 1975; I paid her father a dowry of 100 cows. After our wedding, we settled in our State of Aweil.

Two years after Teresa and I married, on 8 April 1977, we welcomed our first son, Lual Arthur Akuien Chol. I was thrilled to have a son. Two years later, on 3 September 1979, Teresa gave birth to our first daughter, Awut Arthur Akuien Chol. Once again, this delighted me. So did the birth of Deng Arthur Akuien Chol on 24 December 1982.

In Sudan, the custom is for men to marry more than one woman and in 1981, I married Mary Adut Achor Dhel. Mary gave birth to Angok Arthur Akuien Chol on 16 October 1984 and the following year, on 14 September 1985, Teresa gave birth to Akot Arthur Akuien Chol. Two years later, on 17 January 1987, Mary gave birth to Deng Arthur Akuien Chol and in the same year, on 22 February 1987, Teresa delivered another son; we named him Angok Arthur Akuien Chol. Three years later, on 12 November 1990, Teresa and I welcomed Chol Arthur Akuien Chol, then on 12 November 1994, our youngest daughter, Achol Arthur Akuien Chol, was born. All my children made me incredibly happy, and I loved being a father.

The most important thing in life is to have children. As my children grew up, I took them to places children enjoy, such as seeing wild animals at the zoo. We also visited cattle camps so they could learn about our Dinka traditions and see how I grew up. I prioritised education as a first plan for my children and ensured they gained it at all costs. After school, I helped them with their homework, and I played football with them. Being a father brings me great joy. I am tremendously happy to have my children with me and to witness how much they have all grown and achieved. I am now a grandfather of 25 grandchildren, and I also enjoy spending time with them.

Family has always been tremendously important to me and at this age, my children have made me extremely proud; I remain proud of them. Lual, Angok and Akot are graduates of Australian universities and Angok would later join politics and serve in the National Parliament as a nominated Member of Parliament. Akot works in the Bank of South Sudan, which serves as the country's Central Bank, Deng is a senior officer in the security sector's intelligence department and Angok Jnr is a businessman in Juba. Deng Jnr currently lives with me in Juba. My daughter Awut is a banker in Australia and Chol and Achol live in Australia. Seeing my children growing keeps me motivated and grateful to God.

CHAPTER 10

SERVING MY PEOPLE

My first step in seeking election to the Parliament of Sudan was to join William Deng's political party, the Sudan African National Union. Deng had established the party in 1963 with Father Saturnino Ohure and Joseph Oduho when they were both in exile in Uganda. The party contested elections in Sudan seeking autonomy for South Sudan within a federal structure, and in 1968, Deng won his parliamentary seat by a landslide. Tragically, he was assassinated shortly after results were announced.

My family lived in Aweil, in the south-eastern part of Northern Barh el Ghazalan, so I wanted to represent my people from that area. Aweil South had three sections, and a chief administered each of them. Its population was 50,000, mostly subsistence farmers who grew sorghum and raised cattle on swampy grasslands. Most were desperately poor because the area lacked basic infrastructure such as clean drinking water, electricity, schools, health services, roads and rail. My goal was to be their voice in Parliament to get them these services and help them break the entrenched cycle of poverty that continued from one generation to the next.

Aweil is prone to flooding during the wet season, making it difficult to get around because the dirt roads turn to thick, slushy mud. This contributed to poverty in several ways: the lack of clean water and electricity meant girls and women had to spend hours every day trying to navigate waterlogged roads to collect firewood for cooking and water for drinking, cooking and washing. This stopped girls from going to school and women could not do paid work because their days were taken up with chores that would not exist if their villages had a water supply and electricity, let alone good roads and a railway.

Boggy roads made it difficult for children to get to school and adults to travel for paid work. Unnavigable roads also made it almost impossible for farmers to trade their produce or for food and medical supplies to reach the villagers. This contributed to high levels of food insecurity, malnutrition, illness, illiteracy and trapped my people in abject poverty.

The Sudan African National Union had little money for running an election campaign, but our supporters donated as much as they could afford to help us get elected. Using these funds, I appointed campaign workers who mobilised our people to support me and my political agenda. They travelled around Aweil sharing my election promises, which included building a hospital and school in Aweil, good roads and a railway line.

The election campaign was held during the dry season, enabling us to travel around Aweil. We met all the chiefs and villagers, asking them to support me. The chiefs told me everyone in Aweil was proud of me because I was one of the first university graduates from our area; they said they wanted me to represent them in the Parliament.

During the election campaign, each candidate was represented by a symbol and a written name because most people in Aweil were illiterate and could not read a voting form. My symbol was Spear, and my electoral staff told everyone in Aweil to mark it on the election form. On election day in each village, voters chose the symbol representing their preferred candidate, then placed the form in a special box. Electoral officers collected the boxes, took them to a voting centre, then counted the votes. Voting extended over a week to give electoral officers time to visit each village, and counting took another week, so it was a lengthy process.

When I heard I had won the election for my area, I was euphoric. Some of my good friends in Aweil were also elected and the Sudan African National Union won seven seats in the National Parliament. To celebrate, I hosted a big party, and we roasted several bulls.

My cousin Lawrence Lual Lual Akuei also contested the election. During the day, we'd go to the same rallies and talk against each other because we were political opponents. But at night we'd enjoy dinner together. The solidarity and union between us was a principle our people embraced, and it provided an example of how to behave whenever conflict arises. However, political culture has changed for the worse in recent decades and these days opponents consider themselves fierce enemies; I believe it will change in the future.

After I was elected, I travelled to Khartoum to take up my position as the representative of my people in Aweil South. My friends from Aweil also joined me and we agreed to work together to represent our people. My first day in Parliament was momentous. As I sat in the parliamentary chamber, I reflected on all the reasons I returned to Sudan after 10 years in exile and my purpose in life as Arthur Akuien Chol; it was deeply an emotional day.

When I returned to Sudan, the emergence of Islam during my absence troubled me. The continued oppression and marginalisation of our people also worried me deeply. As someone who'd been given the opportunity of an excellent education, I knew I had a responsibility to give our people a voice. I was committed to helping my people break the poverty cycle and experience lives filled with opportunity and hope rather than hunger, malnutrition, illiteracy and despair. My other goals included giving my people access to clean water, electricity, schools, hospitals and health clinics. I was also committed to promoting sustainable farming practices and providing my people with tractors and other modern farming equipment to increase crop yields and income.

On my first day in Parliament, I gave a speech and joined several committees to deal with specific issues. I was extremely happy. Parliament in Khartoum sat from 10 o'clock to two o'clock, then the rest of the time I met with the villagers I represented to help them access health care and food and get their children into school; looking after my people was my priority. The first major projects I started in my area were rehabilitation of Aweil Civil Hospital in Aweil town and the railway line from Khartoum to Aweil that extended to Wau.

CHAPTER 11

MINISTER FOR COMMERCE AND INDUSTRY

In January 1978, after representing my people in Sudan's National Parliament for four years, the Parliament was dissolved, and the country headed to the ballot box. The regional Government of Southern Sudan also held an election, and the people of Aweil again voted for me to be their representative. I felt proud to take my seat in the regional Parliament in Juba and even more so when Abel

Alier appointed me as the Minister for Commerce and Industry.

Later in 1978, oil resources were discovered in the Bentiu area in Southern Sudan and, as Minister for Commerce and Industry, it came under my portfolio. Khartoum set up a board of governors to control the oil reserves and revenues and, although Abel Alier insisted it should include representatives from southern Sudan, it excluded our South Sudanese people. This was disastrous for us because it enabled Khartoum to control all decision-making about oil production and, crucially, revenues; Khartoum ensured Southern Sudan received only a tiny portion of the oil revenues. These were the main triggers for Sudan's second civil war, which started in 1983.

From the beginning, I set out to ensure my people received their share of oil revenues so that the southern regional government could invest in basic infrastructure—electricity, clean drinking water, hospitals, health services, schools, roads and railways—and boost economic development. However, those politicians from the north who opposed The Addis Ababa Agreement and the South's autonomy insisted provincial boundaries be redrawn to enable Bentiu to become part of northern Sudan. This would ensure Khartoum pocketed all the oil revenues.

Our people resolved to never let that happen. Fortunately, after a fierce debate, Southern Sudan members of the National Assembly persuaded Nimeiry to abandon this plan.

As a landlocked nation, South Sudan has no access to the ocean and all imports and exports must go through other countries. This increases the cost of traded goods and reduces revenues flowing to the government. The southern regional government was planning to build an oil refinery in Bentiu to provide training and jobs for our people and boost economic development. But the north's politicians decided to pump crude oil via a 1,700-kilometre-long pipeline from Bentiu to Port Sudan on the Red Sea in the country's north. Their plan was to export the oil to lucrative world markets and to refine oil for domestic use in Kosti, south of Khartoum, while keeping it under the north's control. This meant revenues from the South's rich oil reserves flowed to Khartoum's coffers rather than those of southern Sudan.

Although most of the Sudan's national income derived from the South's oil and other natural resources, the north robbed our people of their fair share of the national cake of development. It even denied Southerners of employment in jobs such as local and provincial administrators, teachers and almost all salaried and employed workers. Instead, northerners stationed in the South Sudan filled these positions. The north also continued to impose Islam on the Christian South. These and other grievances were enough fuel to ginger the South to take up arms to liberate ourselves from the yoke of oppression.

After The Addis Ababa Agreement was signed, Nimeiry appointed Abel Alier as President of the High Executive Council and Sudan's Vice-President. Joseph Lagu was furious because he'd assumed Nimeiry would appoint him in recognition of the central role he played in negotiating the Agreement. This led to bitter rivalry between Lagu and Alier that took on a sharp tribal character. Lagu accused Alier of appointing more ministers from the Dinka tribe than other tribes such as his, the Madi ethnic group of Eastern Equatoria State, and he and his supporters began campaigning for a separate Equatoria Region to escape Dinka domination. Lagu's continued opposition to Alier fuelled deep conflict within the regional government, undermining its efforts to establish political stability, economic growth and peace.

Lagu aligned himself with Nimeiry and northern politicians and advocated for further devolution of power to the southern regional government. He also wanted to weaken Alier's authority and power, hoping Nimeiry would remove Alier and appoint him as the South's leader. Nimeiry saw this as his chance to exploit divisions within the southern regional government. Conflict escalated, weakening and destabilising the regional government, and taking attention away from building the institutions and infrastructure required to advance South Sudan.

Alarmingly, once the regional government was established, Nimeiry kept violating the terms of The Addis Ababa Agreement by intervening in southern politics and interfering with many of Abel Alier's policy initiatives. He also exploited rivalries between southern ethnic groups, enabling him to divide-and-conquer, so much so that the future of The Addis Ababa Agreement was under threat.

During the late 1970s, Southerners' discontent with Alier intensified because of his continued deference to Nimeiry. Southerners demanded that Alier block Nimeiry's interference in their politics and governance, but that was unlikely, because Nimeiry's own political position was at risk, and he was attempting to appease his enemies by undermining the South's autonomy. To protect his presidency, Nimeiry strengthened ties with the increasingly influential Muslim Brotherhood and other radical Islamist groups, and he increasingly imposed

Islam on the South, despite The Addis Ababa Agreement banning it. By 1980, he wore jallabiya in public instead of his usual military uniform and he was seen as more of an *imam*, his attempt to build support among radical Islamist groups and appease his enemies.

Another reason Southerners lost faith in Alier was that Khartoum's promised development funds did not flow to the regional government. The northern politicians who opposed The Addis Ababa Agreement resisted diverting funds from large-scale development projects in the north to the distant 'swampy South'. Other forces undermining Alier's position were systemic corruption within the civil service and continued political and tribal divisions.

Eventually, Alier became more forceful in challenging Nimeiry's decisions and authority, and he took a more active role in economic matters. But this just antagonised northern politicians, who intensified their efforts to dismantle The Addis Ababa Agreement. By 1980, disenchantment with Alier's achievements, combined with Lagu's close connections with northern leaders, enabled Lagu to topple Alier. After he took over the leadership, Lagu appointed me as Minister of Agriculture and Natural Resources in the same year.

As leader of the southern regional government and

Sudan's Vice-President, Lagu continued advocating for further devolution of power to the southern regional government. While Nimeiry agreed with this approach, what he had in mind was to divide the south into three regions to further neutralise its political and financial power, with devastating consequences for our people.

CHAPTER 12

THE TRAGIC STORY OF MY COUNTRY

In June 1983, Nimeiry issued a decree abolishing The Addis Ababa Agreement, the Regional Self-Government Act and all the institutions of government underpinning the agreement. This brought critical economic development projects to a standstill and placed Sudan on the brink of war. Nimeiry also announced his intention to divide the South into its three original regions—Bahr al Ghazal, Upper Nile and Equatoria—because he knew it would be much more difficult for three separate provinces to exert political influence in Khartoum.

Dividing the South into three regions further weakened its autonomy, political power and economic growth. It would also further disintegrate Southerners into tribal groups, which is one of the major problems affecting the people of South Sudan today. Nimeiry insisted all taxes imposed by the regions be sent to Khartoum for redistribution by his government and, of course, he had no intention of returning it to the South equitably. Only a small proportion of the taxes collected in the South were ever returned to the regional government to invest in building a sustainable future for our people of South Sudan.

Disastrously, Nimeiry's decree forced the South back into the unresolved political, social, economic and religious problems of a decade earlier, reversing any gains achieved by the regional government. Clearly, Lagu and Equatoria did not get what they wanted, particularly the ability to keep the taxes they collected.

A few months after dismantling the southern regional government, Nimeiry announced the imposition of new Sharia provisions in the criminal code, including the banning of alcohol and imposition of punishments such as limb amputation. Special courts were set up to enforce

Islamic Law, which applied to the whole of Sudan, including Southerners and Christians. To our horror, growing fears during the 1970s that Khartoum would impose Sharia as the foundation for an Islamic State were finally realised.

By imposing Islam on the South, Nimeiry wilfully ignored our traditional cultures, languages and religions. By then, the South did not have the political power to fight off Nimeiry's imposition of an Islamic State. It did not take us long to realise penalties were being applied disproportionately against Southerners, Christians and westerners, setting the stage for war.

On 16 May 1983, John Garang, a Dinka from a Christian family, responded to Nimeiry's actions by founding the Sudanese People's Liberation Army (SPLA) as a guerrilla movement to fight Khartoum and re-establish an autonomous Southern Sudan. He also launched the Sudanese People's Liberation Movement (SPLM), SPLA's political wing. Libya, Uganda and Ethiopia supported the SPLM/A with funding.

Garang had significant political capital because many northerners and Southerners respected his vision of a 'New Sudan', a Sudan that was united, secular and with equal rights for all. A strong advocate for national unity,

Garang believed that by minorities from all tribes and religions joining together they would have the critical mass to form a majority Sudanese government, with the power to replace both Presidents Nimeiry and later Omar al-Bashir who would in time oust Nimeiry in a bloodless coup de'etat.

Tragically, formation of the SPLA marked the beginning of Sudan's second civil war, a war that would continue for 21 years and be viewed as one of the longest civil wars on record. It would cost millions of my people's lives, leave millions more displaced and vulnerable to human rights abuses, and cause famine, malnutrition and the spread of infectious diseases.

In 1983, Nimeiry appointed me as Sudan's representative at the Arab Maritime Academy in Egypt. The academy was established in 1972 to train students from Arab, African, Asian and European nations in maritime transport, engineering and management sciences and the application of modern technology in these fields. My role was to recruit students for the academy from South Sudan and other African countries. It would, however, take me three years to move to Egypt because of the political situation in the Sudan. By then Garang's vision had already mobilised me, and as a clandestine member, I started communicating with my colleagues who'd joined Garang on an official basis. From then on, my stand was clear: I had to join the liberation struggle of my people once again and would do so by becoming part of the SPLA's internal cell in Khartoum.

Kerbino Kuanyin of battalion 104, started the revolt in Bor on 16th May 1983, followed by William Nyuon Bany from battalion 105. The Southern mutiny had started once again, and it was an enormous blow for Nimeiry. This would prompt him to opt for peaceful measures immediately after witnessing the enormous impact of the new Southern mutiny. Being a career soldier, Nimeiry knew this time the Southerner's revolt was far more organised. Peace talks started, and in 1986 I was among the delegates on the Government's team at Addis Ababa. It was a great opportunity for me and in side meetings, I freely shared insights with Dr John Garang. Already familiar with our internal cell, he was supportive and appreciated our efforts in Khartoum. Garang urged us to keep mobilising while in Khartoum and to seek support that favoured the Southern cause. In fact, it was around this period that Dr Lam Akol, also a delegate, officially declared he was joining the SPLA/SPLM.

Three years after my appointment to Egypt my

family accompanied me and we lived in Alexandria, a Mediterranean port city. While there, I continued to serve in my role as a politician representing my constituents of Aweil, and I frequently communicated with SPLA leaders, including Dr John Garang. It was then I started organising for the SPLM/A, secretly recruiting rebels from Bahr el Ghazal to Equatoria in the south of Sudan to fight. Many of these recruits had returned to South Sudan from exile to join the new movement and fight for our independence. By the end of 1986, the SPLA had over 12,500 soldiers, bringing me great joy then that continues today because it inspired me and other south Sudanese to continue our fight while we lived in neighbouring countries.

Six years after arriving in Egypt, I was recalled to Sudan because the Government of Sudan suspected me of collaborating with Garang. It was time for me to take an open stand, and I began planning to join the SPLM on an official basis. I began communicating with my political colleague and good friend Dr Justin Yaac Arop, as well as Commander Lual Diing Wol. In 1992, I travelled to Kenya to meet Dr John Garang. Dr Justin Yaac facilitated my visit and would later become a powerful ally until his demise in 2008. His death was unexpected and left an enormous vacuum.

Being an economist and having had experience with the government in Khartoum, I understood the financial cost of war diverted scarce resources away from economic development in the South and building a sustainable future for my people. This troubles me deeply, particularly because it robbed generations of children from the opportunity of being educated, trapping them and their families in desperate poverty. It also deprived our country of educated leaders who could navigate Sudan's complex political, social, economic and religious issues and build a peaceful, stable future for my people. My understanding of these issues encouraged me to continue fighting for my people and gave me courage in my meetings with Dr John Garang.

During the late 1980s, ethnic rivalries escalated within the SPLM and SPLA leadership group that would take tribal shaping, principally between the Dinka community led by John Garang, and the Nuer, headed by rebel leader Dr Riak Machar. The principal source of conflict was disagreement about the movement's goals. Garang initially advocated for a secular, democratic, united Sudan in which Southerners achieved full representation, whereas Machar insisted on a fully independent South Sudan. Machar mobilised the Nuer against Garang because he wanted to replace him as SPLM/A leader. The conflict dragged on for years.

In 1991, the Nuer people moved back to their ancestral lands in the Upper Nile and once there, they started ambushing Dinka fighters on their journey to Ethiopia. Machar defected from the SPLM/A and tried to gain support from the Sudanese government. He formed a splinter group, SPLA-Nasir, which led violent and ethnically motivated attacks against the SPLM with the help of oil revenues and weapons covertly supplied by Khartoum. The Nation's leaders in Khartoum took advantage of these divisions by adopting deliberate divide-and-conquer policies to keep control over my people.

Eventually Machar's forces lost both the physical and ideological war. His political movement was divided, and he sought refuge in the north. When he failed to get what he wanted from Khartoum, he returned to the south to negotiate his way back into the leadership of the SPLM under Garang.

On returning to the fold, Macher demanded to be Vice-President to Garang. During one of his many absences from the movement's base, Garang appointed Salva Kiir, a Dinka from a different region of Bhar el Gazal to him, as his Vice-President. But Machar had his eye firmly on the position as a representative of the Nuer tribe. Garang said this was not possible because he and Macher were both from the Upper Nile and the President and Vice-President could not come from the same region.

Garang called a meeting to discuss the leadership. At the meeting, James Wani Igga, third-ranked in the SPLM, gave up his position to Machar to keep the peace. That resulted in Machar becoming third in command; Kiir remained Vice-President.

Ultimately, conflict within the SPLM/A resulted in it splitting into three dominant factions: the SPLA Torit faction led by Garang; the SPLA Bahr al Ghazal faction led by Kerbino Kuanyin Bol; and the South Sudan Independence Movement led by Machar. I stood firm with the leadership of Garang and travelled around Aweil to urge my people in Northern Bhar El Gazal State to support him. Some of Aweil's leaders who backed Garang were Lual Lual Akuey, Lual Diing Wol, Aldo Ajou Deng, Dau Atorjong, George Kuac, Malong Awan, Chour Deng Mareng, Ajongo Mawut, Madut Biar Yel, Santino Deng Wol, Santo Ayang Deng and Butrus Bol Bol, to name a few.

Regrettably, internal divisions within SPLM and SPLA distracted its leaders from focusing on its primary goal, achieving independence for Southern Sudan and our people. Rather than concentrating on defeating the north, fighting among the South's different factions paralysed decision-making and wasted scarce financial resources that should have been used to fuel economic growth and improve living standards. John Garang tried his best to unite the movement, but his attempts failed because the bitter rivalries were so entrenched.

CHAPTER 13

CHAIRMAN OF HUMANITARIAN AFFAIRS

In April 1994, John Garang tried to defuse internal clashes and unite our movement by organising the National Convention of New Sudan. The convention was held in the bush in the SPLA-liberated area of Chukudum in Equatoria. It attracted over 500 supporters, many of whom walked to Chukudum, from three regions of South Sudan—Equatoria, Upper Nile and Bahr el Ghazal—who agreed on a system of governance for the SPLM.

One of Garang's priorities for the convention was agreement on the issue of separatism and the unity of Sudan. For several years, Garang had advocated for a 'New Sudan' characterised by a united, secular Sudan, but by the time of the convention, he accepted a shift in SPLM policy towards incorporating separatist demands. In Chukudum, SPLM members agreed to define 'New Sudan' as applying to liberated areas under the control of SPLM/A.

It was also agreed that 'New Sudan' would be governed by three branches of government: legislative, executive and judicial. A system of local governments comprising five levels was also formalised—boma, payam, county, region and central—and five regional administrations of 'New Sudan' were created: Bahr el Ghazal, Equatoria, Southern Blue Nile, Southern Kordofan and Upper Nile.

During the convention, our supporters elected a new National Liberation Council/National Executive Committee of SPLM/A with John Garang as Chairman and Salva Kiir Mayardit as a Deputy Chairman. One of their responsibilities was directing the SPLA in its fight with the north for independence. I was elected as a member of the National Liberation Council and Garang appointed me as Chairman of Humanitarian Affairs for the South Sudan Relief and Rehabilitation Commission, 'SRRA', in Yei and northern Kenya.

During the civil war, my role was to mobilise, deliver and supervise food and relief supplies from our foreign partners to war-affected areas of Upper Nile and Bar el Gazal in Southern Sudan by airlifting pallets of food from Kenya. The commission had the authority to issue travel documents and repatriated displaced South Sudanese from refugee camps across East Africa to liberated areas of South Sudan. Our friends in neighbouring countries provided financial support to the commission to enable it to continue its relief efforts.

To ensure the smooth flow of relief supplies, I regularly visited areas where food was being distributed, and stationed officials across the Upper Nile and Equatoria to report on the food distribution project in SPLM-controlled areas. But forces loyal to the government of Sudan, Riek Machar's militia, regularly attacked the areas where food was being distributed, so we depended on the diplomatic clout of the World Food Program, UNICEF and America to force Khartoum to cease and desist.

In 1997 after I'd served as Chairman of Humanitarian Affairs for four years, John Garang asked me to take over management of the movement's finances from James

Wani Igga, who is now South Sudan's Vice-President. Garang told me he'd keenly followed my efforts as head of the humanitarian program, and my contribution impressed him. It made me feel happy my hard work was being noticed. I felt honoured to serve my people as SPLM's Secretary of Finance and was confident I could make significant headway on several development projects. As Secretary of Finance, I funded SPLM bodies across Southern Sudan to enable them to pursue the activities needed to liberate the South.

Meanwhile, peace negotiations continued to end the second civil war and on 21 April 1997, the government of Sudan signed the Khartoum Peace Agreement with the South's militia leaders, including the SPLM. The South Sudan United Democratic Salvation Front, the Union of Sudan African Parties, the Equatoria Defence Force and the South Sudan Independents Group also signed the agreement, which stated:

'We the parties to the conflict in the Sudan:
- Deeply committed to an immediate end to the current armed conflict through peaceful and political means
- Aware that the attainment of a just and lasting peace requires courage, statesmanship, political daring and challenging vision from the parties

- Aware that only a sustainable peace based on justice, equality, democracy, and freedom can lead to a meaningful development and progress which would assist in the solution of the fundamental problems of the people of the Sudan.
- Fully cognizant of the fact that the unity of the Sudan cannot be based on force or coercion, but on the free will of the people
- Hereby agree to make and abide by this agreement.'

The agreement included religious, political and human rights and freedoms, power sharing arrangements between the north and south of the nation, equitable revenue sharing, rehabilitation of war-affected areas and reconciliation. It stated a Coordinating Council in Southern States would be established during an interim period of four years to coordinate and supervise socioeconomic planning, confidence building, peace-nurturing, policy-making and political mobilisation. Riak Machar was appointed to head the council. The SPLA did not sign the Khartoum Peace Agreement and afterwards, the level of conflict escalated to new heights. Ironically, the north funded its attacks on the South with revenues gained from the South's oil.

Meanwhile, the north's political leaders rejected Machar's lobbying for them to support the South's self-determination under his leadership, so he began negotiations with Garang about returning to the SPLA/SPLM as number two in the leadership team. In 2002, Garang allowed Machar to return, but as a senior SPLA commander, the third man in the leadership team, rather than Machar's coveted second position. After Machar's return, SPLM members focused on trying to get things back in order, although I did not trust Machar to genuinely support Garang.

It was a sensitive situation, so I could not say anything about my concerns because my colleagues might have perceived it wrongly. I knew voicing my doubts about Machar's loyalty would cause further conflict and instability within SPLM, so I just had to accept that Macher was back in the leadership team and there was nothing I could do about it.

CHAPTER 14

A FRAGILE PEACE

During the early 2000s, peace talks continued between southern rebels and the Sudanese government on ending the civil war. Finally, a breakthrough occurred in Kenya in 2002 when a set of principles known as the Machakos Protocol was signed. Opposing groups agreed to restart the peace process in Sudan and agreed on principles about the separation of state and religion, structures of governance, a broad power and wealth-sharing framework, and a constitutional review process to guarantee fundamental human and political rights.

The Machakos Protocol also noted future discussions would seek to agree on a comprehensive ceasefire and a plan for repatriation, resettlement, rehabilitation and reconstruction of the war-affected areas. I organised funding for SPLM members to travel to Machakos in Kenya to take part in the peace talks surrounding creation of the Protocol.

From 2001, George Bush was US President, and he threw his support behind moves for a political settlement of Sudan's second civil war. So did African member-countries of Intergovernmental Authority on Development (IGAD), who took the initiative and called for peace talks between the government of Sudan and the SPLM. The talks were held in Kenya and discussions continued for two years.

This involved negotiating and signing six documents:

1. The *Machakos Protocol* of July 2002
2. The *Agreement on Security Arrangements* of September 2003
3. The *Agreement on Wealth-Sharing* of January 2004
4. The *Protocol on Power Sharing* of May 2004
5. The *Protocol on the Resolution of Conflict in Southern Kordofan and Blue Nile States* of May 2004

6. The *Protocol on the Resolution of Conflict in the Abyei Area* of May 2004.

On 9 January 2005, this process culminated in the singing of the Comprehensive Peace Agreement (CPA) in Nairobi by Dr John Garang and the Vice-President of Sudan, Dr Omer Mohamed Taha. The US, Britain, Italy and Norway witnessed the CPA's signing. The CPA embodied Garang's vision of the 'New Sudan', with power sharing between the SPLM and National Congress Party. It included a permanent ceasefire, ending two decades of civil war, autonomy for the South, and revenue and power sharing between the north and South. One of the Agreement's major provisions was to give the people of South Sudan a chance to determine their own future through a referendum, which was to be held after a period of five years.

CHAPTER 15

SOUTH SUDAN'S FIRST MINISTER OF FINANCE

Signing the Comprehensive Peace Agreement ended the two-decade long civil war, bringing peace to Sudan and establishing Southern autonomy. Afterwards, SPLM delegations and emissaries travelled to all parts of Sudan to share details of the Agreement with the Sudanese people. The delegation also prepared our people to welcome John Garang as Sudan's First Vice-President of Sudan.

Afterwards, the delegations returned to Southern Sudan's headquarters in Rumbek to prepare for Garang's inauguration. I met with the head of the delegation to discuss the funding needed for this historic occasion and negotiated with the north to provide funding; the South contributed US$270,000 and the central government of Sudan contributed the rest.

On 9 July 2005 in Khartoum, Dr John Garang, who had spent decades advocating for national unity, signed a power sharing constitution with President Omar al-Bashir. That day he was also inaugurated as Sudan's First-Vice-President and President of South Sudan, the second most powerful position in Sudan. No Christian or southerner had ever held such a high government post. Garang's philosophy of national unity was based on the New Sudan being secular and multi-ethnic. To achieve cohesion, he urged the people of Sudan to embrace all cultures, transcend ethnic and religious factions, and unify under the characteristic they all shared, being Sudanese.

Leaders from neighbouring countries attended the inauguration and Mr Kofi Annan, the UN Secretary-General, was a special guest. About six million Sudanese thronged to Khartoum for the event. After the ceremony, Garang congratulated the Sudanese people: 'This is not my peace or the peace of al-Bashir, it is the peace of the Sudanese people.' This famous quote reminds all Sudanese, particularly Southerners, of the years of struggle.

A few days after his inauguration, John Garang appointed me as Minister for Finance, and I took my oath of office in the forest with other cabinet ministers. That day was a high point in my life and one I will always remember. Shortly after Garang handed me my commission, I walked into my office. It was almost bare, but I knew South Sudan was a new country starting from scratch, so I did not expect to find a well-furnished office with everything in place. As our new nation's first Finance Minister, I was confronted with a mountain of what felt like insurmountable challenges. Still, while I felt the full weight of my responsibility, I did not despair because I was confident that with proper planning, hard work, and a can-do attitude, South Sudan could take giant strides. My thoughts were on how we would chart a development path that would enable our new nation to catch up and be on par with our neighbours.

The next step in our journey towards nationhood was for the SPLM/SPLA leadership to establish and proclaim the independent Government of South Sudan. However, before this took place, Garang made a whirlwind trip to neighbouring Uganda to confer with President Yoweri Museveni and several foreign envoys from Europe and America. After the meeting, on 31 July 2005, Garang jumped into a helicopter owned by a Ugandan company for the night flight home to South Sudan. Tragically, the chopper crashed in bushes, killing Garang and his aides.

A search party found the helicopter's wreckage the following day; sadly, no-one survived. The bodies were retrieved, then flown to Rumbek. Shortly after Garang's death was confirmed, the Vice-President Salva Kiir Mayardit was named as First Vice-President of Sudan and President of South Sudan; Riak Machar was to be Vice-President of South Sudan. Then Kiir travelled with Garang's casket to towns and villages around South Sudan so our people could pay their last respects. Afterwards, Kiir accompanied Garang's remains to Juba for burial.

Garang's widow, the South Sudanese politician Rebecca Nyandeng De Mabior, promised to continue his work: 'In our culture we say: "If you kill the lion, you see what the lioness will do."' General Kiir appointed Rebecca De Mabior as the Minister of Roads and Transport for the Government of South Sudan, and she continued to advocate for full implementation of the Comprehensive Peace Agreement.

After Garang's burial, Kiir came back to Rumbek to prepare for his swearing-in ceremony. Immediately on his return from Khartoum, he named his cabinet, appointing me as Minister of Finance and Economic Planning in the new Government of South Sudan. Deeply saddened by John Garang's death, I resolved to work hard to realise his vision of a New Sudan, one based on freedom of religion, equality, democracy and social justice.

My first action as Finance Minister was to open bank accounts in Kenya and the Bank of Sudan in Khartoum. Then I set to work studying several reports, preparing the newly appointed cabinet's first budget and planning several major initiatives to improve the South's infrastructure and economy. Preparing South Sudan's budget was a heartbreaking task. The reports revealed the South lagged in almost every measure of human development, the result of 21 years of civil war that had consumed billions of dollars. It did not take me long to discover the military absorbed the biggest share of revenues, reducing the funds available for building vital infrastructure and boosting economic and social development.

A pressing concern was finding qualified people to work in the Ministry. This was challenging because there were so few skilled economists and other finance professionals in the South, one outcome of the civil war that thwarted the South's ability to educate its children and young people. Initially, I recruited officials from around Sudan and Kenya, but there were not enough of them, so I negotiated with the Central Bank of Kenya for it to train Southern Sudanese in finance and banking. The program began with 30 candidates, who studied banking in Kenya for 12 months. Most of the candidates were Southern Sudanese who were working in banks in northern Sudan. Other trainees were drawn from what had passed as SPLM's Finance Ministry.

The lack of schools concerned me deeply because one of the major problems confronting our newly independent nation was illiteracy. Insecurity during the civil wars forcibly shut down schools in the South, as I had experienced as a 13-year-old when the mutiny in Torit forced all schools to close for 12 months. Forty years later, South Sudan's education system was at a standstill. It meant our children were out of school, and an entire generation of Southern Sudanese did not have the opportunity of a quality education. That was a complete disaster, and its implications and consequences were too dire to contemplate.

My chief concern was worrying how Southern Sudan

would achieve self-determination or independence without educated leaders to run national and local government administrations. This problem kept me awake at night and reinforced my gratitude to Waa, William Deng, Reverend Atak and all and all the people who enabled made to receive an excellent education, an opportunity I longed to provide for all my people.

As well as paralysing our education system, the civil war and continued conflict between factions within the SPLM had distracted our leaders from developing the roads, utility services, hospitals and electricity our people needed to transition from poverty to sustainable futures. My vow was to focus on building infrastructure as a priority.

Another problem holding back economic growth was the lack of a seaport in South Sudan because it is landlocked. This meant every item imported or exported had to be transported from a neighbouring country's port by land. And that is expensive. We had to think hard about how to overcome this hurdle and learn from Zimbabwe, Mali, Niger, Chad and Burkina Faso that are also landlocked. I wanted to know how these nations handled imports and exports and promoted international trade. The obvious solution was to build good relationships with neighbouring countries such as Kenya, Tanzania and Uganda because our imports and exports passed through their lands to overseas destinations. My goal was to gain their cooperation by negotiating then signing binding trade agreements.

Shortly after starting my new role, I contacted the African Union in Addis Ababa, Ethiopia, a continental organisation I hoped would urge international development agencies and South Sudan's development partners to build a network of roads and railway lines to connect landlocked South Sudan to seaports in neighbouring countries in East Africa. One option was to build a dry port in Juba, South Sudan's capital city. Finding ways to overcome these teething problems was a real headache for our country's new leadership team, but I felt optimistic we could succeed if everyone pulled together. How wrong was I?

Another vital project was setting up units within the Ministry, such as the Department of Planning. One of these sub-departments was procurement, which handled all government purchases. All items and services that needed to be purchased had to pass through it. The system worked efficiently because I brought in advisers from the World Bank. The Ministry established a Customs Department with units at the land borders with neighbouring countries. Border guards and customs officers were brought in from Sudan, re-trained in Yei, then posted to various stations.

South Sudan is a rich country because of its abundance of natural resources such as oil, rich agricultural lands, minerals, forests and fresh water. However, apart from oil drilling, commercialisation of these resources was under-developed. This was a wasted opportunity. Despite our blessings from God in terms of natural resources, revenue collection was suboptimal because of corruption. Most collected revenues were not remitted to government accounts. Instead, they ended up in the pockets of corrupt officials. I estimated that about 40 percent of all revenue reached the government; the remaining 60 percent found its way into private pockets.

Corruption meant our government often could not afford to pay the salaries of public servants and essential workers such as teachers, nurses and civil administrators. It also depleted our development funds. I regularly dismissed officers who were corrupt and employed new officers, but my efforts made little change because newly hired officials would quickly find ways of lining their pockets. The bleeding of government revenue persists to this day.

Another major impediment to the efficient and smooth running of the country was lack of accountability; public accountability is almost non-existent in South Sudanese society. Since the territory won self-government, no public institution or official has been called upon to account for its role or stewardship. Auditing of state institutions is almost unheard of, and no corrupt official has faced a law court. The ongoing conflict between the President and Vice-Presidents is also deeply troubling. Needless to say, such a scenario is unhealthy for Sudan's development.

South Sudan's oil fields contributed 60 percent of the nation's total revenues. Under the Comprehensive Peace Agreement, it was agreed that oil revenues would be distributed equally between South Sudan and Sudan. But I insisted on changing this because a 1,500-kilometre-long pipeline transported the oil northwards from Heglig to Port Sudan. The South paid pipeline fees to the Sudan government, which reduced the percentage of revenues remitted to South Sudan. It was my responsibility to protect the oil revenues we did receive, and I kept them under my watchful eye in the Central Bank of Sudan. My goal was for the funds to be used to establish South Sudan as an independent country.

Worryingly, non-oil revenue was not collected

effectively, and taxes collected by various government agencies did not make it into the government's chest. When other ministries and departments collected taxes, they used them for their own activities. I issued an ultimatum that all taxes collected must be transferred to the Central Treasury and instructed Ministry of Finance officials to visit every tax collecting Ministry to reinforce this message, but no-one heeded my call. Added to that, collecting bodies used their own receipts rather than the ones provided to them by my Ministry.

In South Sudan's first budget, a portion of oil revenues was allocated to reconstructing the roads and highways destroyed during the civil war. The plan was to construct an 809-kilometre highway from El Obeid in the north to Aweil in the South through northern Bahar El Gazal. It would continue on from Aweil to Wau and include several bridges. A network of roads and bridges linking remote towns and villages within the South was also planned.

In 2006, I issued a contract to the company, Ayat, under engineer Abdul Aziz, to build this vital infrastructure. Eventually, Ayat also built roads from Wau to Rumbek in Equatoria, Western Bahar el Gazal and other parts of South Sudan. Building these transport networks created jobs, improved the movement of people and traded goods within Sudan, and boosted economic growth. It was a successful program, and I am proud of what the Ministry achieved.

Unfortunately, internal divisions about SPLM's direction deepened after Garang's death. One source of internal conflict involved Paulino Matip's forces, the most powerful militia from the South that opposed the SPLA during the civil war. Between 1998 and 2003, the north had provided Matip's forces with weapons and ammunition for its fight against the SPLA. After Garang died, Matip successfully negotiated a return to the SPLM leadership as SPLA Deputy Commander-in-Chief. Afterwards, 50,000 of his militia integrated with the SPLA. However, tension remained high, resulting in incomplete reintegration of anti-SPLA forces into the SPLA.

Another issue fuelling internal divisions was that President Salva Kiir Mayardit was a career soldier rather than a politician, something that would profoundly affect my future and that of my family. Unfortunately, the pursuit of a 'New Sudan' lost the priority it received under Garang's leadership. An added concern was that Garang's close advisers and confidants were replaced by Salva Kiir's local supporters, who did not share the same commitment to implementing the Comprehensive Peace

Agreement. This weakened the South's negotiating position with the north about vital aspects of the agreement. The result was escalating tension and infighting between Garang loyalists and the President and less focus on promoting democracy, social justice and equality.

After Matip's return and integration of his forces into the SPLA, I prepared a budget for uniforms, arms, vehicles and food. Integration was difficult because his forces were militia who needed orientation, training and discipline. Also, his demands were expensive because he insisted the Southern Sudan Government treat him the same way as the Government of Sudan had treated him, including expensive cars and a government house to accommodate his wives and many children. The government also paid for travel and medical check-ups in neighbouring countries.

Still, in the months following the signing of the Comprehensive Peace Agreement, my people shared a hope that Sudan would transform into a peaceful nation. Sudanese people moved freely around the country, international companies and investors arrived to build businesses, and trade increased. Critically, the permanent cease fire enabled displaced South Sudanese people to return from exile to their place of origin without fear of being attacked by militia.

Although my role was challenging, I experienced several high points. One was the day I stood up in the Parliament of South Sudan to deliver my first budget statement. I was excited and tremendously happy, but sad Waa, who had died in 1989, was not there to see me being sworn in. But I was pleased my wife Mary Adut and son Deng witnessed this pivotal moment in my life. My wife Teresa Awien was in Australia at the time with my children, but later that year they returned to South Sudan to join me.

Another highlight occurred on 9 March 2006 at the first meeting of the Sudan Consortium in Paris when I presented progress reports and future plans on budget, financial and aid management. The Consortium, which was organised by the United Nations, International Monetary Fund and World Bank, brought together delegates from the Government of National Unity, the Government of Southern Sudan, and about 130 international partners, including eight ministers of international development. Salva Kiir Mayardit led the Sudanese delegation of 12 ministers.

The Sudan Consortium aimed to increase national and international funding for economic and social development in Sudan. The principal issue we discussed was the economic, structural and institutional reform required to increase the transparency of government budgets and ensure rigorous governance. Delegates also reviewed progress on implementing the Comprehensive Peace Agreement and planned future actions to consolidate peace and address poverty and dislocation among the Sudanese people.

At the end of the two-day meeting, delegates agreed sound progress had been made on implementing the Comprehensive Peace Agreement, but much more must be achieved on the ground to promote economic development. Critically, the International Monetary Fund, World Bank and several international governments and agencies demanded that Sudan's leaders improve transparency and accountability and introduce a policy of zero tolerance to corruption, a requirement I wholeheartedly supported.

Despite the myriad of deeply entrenched systemic challenges the Finance Ministry faced, it introduced several development programs to improve South Sudan's economy and the wellbeing of my people. This pleased me immensely, but I knew our efforts had barely scratched the surface. Resolving South Sudan's entrenched economic, social and political issues would require a lifetime of focused intervention; I resolved to do everything in my power to achieve this goal.

CHAPTER 16

TREACHERY

To my great distress, in 2006, I was accused of corruption and misusing and stealing public funds during the first two years of our transitional regional government, an allegation I vehemently deny. These accusations began after Omar al-Bashir visited Juba and, while at a public rally, he mentioned giving the Government of South Sudan US$60,000,000. To my surprise, Salva Kiir asked me where these funds were, yet he knowingly gave directives on expenditures when the funds were released shortly after Garang's death. After reporting back to the President and mentioning giving Pagan Amum US$30,000,000, my turbulent political encounters would begin. Pagan Amum was the SPLM Secretary-General at that time; he received the funds in the Party's name through his personal account. A fact I maintain to this day.

Like me, Sudanese citizens and the media were vocal in their support of improved transparency and accountability, and it outraged them to hear of these allegations. Over the following months, public pressure to dismiss me as Minister for Finance and Economic Planning intensified, and in 2007, it had escalated to the point that President Salva Kiir Mayardit removed me from his cabinet. That day in 2007 was one of my darkest; I will never forget it.

I believe the driving force for accusations against me was that the new SPLM leadership team was dominated by soldiers turned political leaders who had a different vision to the late John Garang. Their goal was to speedily enrich themselves through the public coffers. I was an economist and politician rather than a soldier and my friendship with Garang had started at Rumbek Senior Secondary School; we were close allies. He respected me for my achievements in managing SPLM's humanitarian affairs and finances, and I was popular among his supporters.

Pagan and the SPLM's military leaders did not want dissent from people like me who supported Garang's vision of a New Sudan, so their solution was to defame me to prompt my dismissal from the cabinet and ultimately, the SPLM. There were no grounds for accusing me of corruption and crucially, no evidence to support their claims. Instead, it was a deliberate attempt to get rid of me from SPLM so the movement's leaders could pursue their own agenda.

The officials I stopped from pocketing the government money they coveted engineered the accusations and my arrest, and I was forced to endure house arrest for several months. This was deeply distressing for me and my family. The government also stopped paying my salary, and I was not allowed to represent my people.

Immediately, I started preparing a comprehensive report to the Public Accounts Committee, but it was difficult to do this under house arrest because I did not have ready access to crucial documents. But I was fortunate that some loyal colleagues brought me much of the evidence I needed to verify my innocence. At the time, I did not refute the allegations publicly for reasons of patriotism. Too much internal conflict already existed within the SPLM, and I did not want to heighten tensions by accusing the true culprits, several SPLM colleagues, of corruption.

I had introduced strict rules to stop officials lining their own pockets with government money and in retaliation, some colleagues were trying to discredit and defame me. If I spoke out with my claims, it would have undermined the independence process my people and I had fought so hard to achieve; I preferred to remain silent, believing it was the right approach given the critical stage of our independence negotiations.

That was the beginning of my downfall because certain unscrupulous, corrupt individuals within the governing system wanted to maintain easy access to public money without the fear of me questioning them. My goal had always been to eradicate the systemic corruption perpetrated by these individuals, enabling us to invest oil revenues into building infrastructure, promoting economic growth and providing opportunities for my people to break free of crippling poverty.

False allegations that I stole money from the Government of Southern Sudan have forced me and my family to endure immense personal suffering, public suspicion and abuse. These allegations are a personal attack against my integrity and reflect on the integrity of my family, who have suffered in silence while protesting my innocence. I am blessed to have such a supportive, loving family who trusts me and believes in my innocence.

In 2010, the SPLM told me I could not represent the movement at the election that year, so I contested it as an independent candidate. Disappointingly, I lost to Dr Belario Ahoy Ngong. The SPLM established an electoral college, and I was dismissed on grounds of being unpopular because being electable was a fundamental requirement. This was a constituency I had represented and served for over four decades, and I was not shocked because I understood the political turmoil. The following year, after South Sudan gained Independence, President Salva Kiir nominated me to serve in the Council of States, the Upper House of South Sudan's Parliament, to represent my people in Northern Bahr el Ghazal.

To this day, my conscience remains crystal clear, so I am not afraid of fighting to prove my innocence, even if that means going on trial at the age of 80 years old. I still urge the government as a matter of urgency to conduct a thorough, transparent investigation. I am confident this will disclose the full facts and truth behind the discrepancies and expose the corrupt individuals at the centre of the missing funds.

CHAPTER 17

DECLARING MY INNOCENCE

On 8 February 2012, South Sudan's Auditor General Stephen Wondu presented a report to the National Assembly indicating 'huge financial irregularities' during 2005 and 2006. The report recommended prosecution of all those involved, including me. The following day, I fronted the media at the Home and Away Hotel in Juba to declare my innocence. I also issued the following media release:

09/02/2012

**Press Release from Hon. Arthur Akuien Chol,
South Sudan Former Finance Minister Fired For Corruption**

On behalf of the South Sudanese citizens, the leadership of South Sudan, and my own behalf, I wish to take this opportunity to thank all the sons and daughters of this newborn nation and congratulate them all for a job well done in ensuring our independence as a new nation. I would also extend my warm appreciation to the leadership of our President, General Salva Kiir Mayardit for leading us through the hardships and delivering us to our new country. My appearance today before you all is in the sole interest of all citizens of this country, the Republic of South Sudan, whom I remain loyal to.

As you all know, I was the first Minister of Finance and Economic Planning for the Government of South Sudan, a position I held through the era of struggle, up until 2007, when I was dismissed, due to false allegations of corruption that were made against me. Today marks my first public appearance in reference to this matter as I have never spoken out since my removal from office. The reason why I have never publicly stood up and countered the allegations was for reasons of patriotism. I did not want to spoil the process that was leading us, as the people known as the "Southern Sudanese", to the independence of South Sudan and the declaration of the Republic of South Sudan as a united nation.

I was accused recently in the newspapers, and by some Parliamentarians, of not going to Parliament to answer questions about the irregularities in the 2006 report produced by the Auditor General. The reason why I was not present at that meeting was because I was told that my presence was not required as I had already written and submitted a report to the Public Accounts Committee.

As I have noted, there have been constant attempts being made by some few individuals within the current governing body to discredit and defame me as a significant figure among the founding members of this nation. These accusations all range from my time in office and continue to this date.

It is becoming more and more apparent that there are those, who no longer wish to be the sleeping dogs, but who would rather prefer for me to throw a snake among them and see which ones run, and which ones get bitten.

It is unfortunate that I have been pushed to the point where it is necessary for me to take this opportunity to list out some, if only a few of the transgressions by a few against the public interest of the People of South Sudan, for, as I mentioned earlier, time has now allowed me to speak out and let the whole country know how public funds were and are being mishandled and misused.

1. In 2006, I was accused of misusing and stealing public funds. This was propagated by some few individuals within the government, leading to a caucus sitting of the Sudan People's Liberation Movement (SPLM) as an intervention. The latter in response to this matter resolved with their own clear findings of the transparency and accountability that existed within what was then, my Ministry. In my own opinion, this was the beginning of my downfall. The government of the period of 2005-06, had a great influx of cash, and I being the Minister of Finance at that time, had strict operative values, that could not allow public money to be rotating anyhow among corrupt individuals. This was the beginning of my accusations by a manipulation of opinion, both Government and public, used as a way for me to be impeached in order to allow a certain few unscrupulous and corrupt individuals within the governing system easy access to public money without the fear of question by me.

2. In the same year of 2006, I was again accused on matters regarding a grant of $60,000,000 (Sixty million US dollars) given to GOSS by the President of Sudan, Omar al-Bashir. These accusations were made by the SPLM Secretary-General, Pagan Amum, and Luka Biong, stating that I had stolen the above figures but clearly, this amount was paid to the account of GOSS in the Bank of Sudan with Issac Makur and Silvano Jal Malith as signatories to the account. My involvement in this could be in reference to the approvals I made, having instructions from above, leading to the expenditure of $30,000,000, of which I hold copies of all documents of their expenditures. The other $30,000,000 are in the hands of SPLM SG, Pagan Amum, as I paid it directly into his account on instructions from above. I believe he can clearly tell the public how he spent those funds.

3. Leading to my impeachment as the Minister of Finance, I was accused of purchasing vehicles from Cardinal Company at a price twice the actual amount. These vehicles were purchased following instructions from the Vice-President of GOSS, Dr Riak Machar Teny, that I should purchase the vehicles from Cardinal Company for various ministries. In turn, I directed

the Undersecretary of Finance to proceed following the procurement procedures. I was then held responsible for this purchase while my directives to the undersecretary clearly indicated procurement procedures. As a result, I was relieved of my duties as Minister of Finance, and immediately accused and arrested for corruption. I was later investigated and tried but there was no evidence of wrongdoing and the case was dismissed by the province judge in Juba.

4. Leading up to the final accusation, which is the driving factor of holding this press conference today. These accusations have been directly made by an individual who has turned to the media to show grievances of his dismissal as the Governor of Bank of South Sudan. For instance, I was tasked by the Auditor General to explain why transfer of oil revenue from GONU to GOSS was done through Geneva-based bank accounts. In response, I clearly stated that there was a transfer made by Mr Malok, the then Governor of BOSS. This transfer was made without my knowledge or consent, and when I discovered the transfer, I wrote to the Governor of the Bank of Sudan to return the funds to our account in the Bank of Sudan and for Mr Malok to explain why he did the transfer. I think

he should be held accountable and explain why he did that and on whose authority. To this day, I have never received a reply, other than a vendetta being waged against me to discredit me and have me impeached for corruption.

As the facts of this case are to be exposed, then let it be known that Elijah Malok, who was at that time, the Governor of the Bank of Southern Sudan, and as such, he had no authority over the Government Finances and the allocation of Government money, but he was a custodian of Government accounts, yet, it was he himself accompanied by two colleagues, who went to Geneva and opened an account in the name, and on behalf of the Government of Southern Sudan, this being done without the knowledge, or the authorisation of myself, as the then Minister of Finance of GOSS. The only authorised officials then and now, in the Ministry of Finance who are authorised to take such action, are the Undersecretary of Finance and the Director-General of Accounts. By having taken this action, the then Governor of BOSS, completely violated the laws governing the guardianship of the public Finances of the BOSS.

Having discovered that this action had been taken and

that wrong procedures had been adopted, I had to intervene on behalf of GOSS to retrieve the public money and ensure that it was returned to the account of the rightful owner, that being the account of GOSS in the Bank of Southern Sudan. In fact, that outward transaction by the then Governor of BOSS Mr Elijah Malok, was a flagrant act of attempted theft, and if I had not discovered the illegal transaction and insisted that it be returned, it would probably have become a *fait accomplis*, and the money would have been lost and never recovered by GOSS. Is it conceivable that I am accused of corruption because I made sure the money came home to where it belonged, by the same people that took it out illegally?

In conclusion, however, I do acknowledge and commend the Auditor General for having tabled the audit reports for the year 2005-2006 before the National Assembly, however, I do not believe that there was sufficient attention given to the discovery of the true facts and that a lot of preconceived assumptions were just taken for granted. In light of the current oil crisis and the austerity measures undertaken by the Government of South Sudan, I strongly recommend that proper investigations be carried out to determine actual truths to the matter at hand.

These false allegations that have been made against me,

have caused me and my family to endure a great amount of personal suffering, public suspicion and abuse, and is widely reported on the internet that I have stolen money from the Government of Southern Sudan. This is a personal attack against my integrity, and in turn, reflects on the integrity of my family, who has suffered in silence, while protesting my innocence. I let it be known, that for the sake of this Nation and from the time I was appointed as the guardian of the Nation's finances, I guarded them well, and I thank the late Dr John Garang Mabior and his excellency Salva Kiir Mayardit for having entrusted me with the guardianship of the Nation's finances up to and beyond the CPA in 2005 up to 2007. After the death of the late Dr John Garang Mabior, it appears to me that there are conspirators and corrupt individuals who were able to rise to high positions of leadership. I am sorry that the former Governor of the Bank of Southern Sudan and the Secretary-General of the SPLM were able to seize the leadership and high position, something which I am sure that the 98% of the people in this country who voted for separation in the referendum cannot and will not accept.

I take this opportunity to inform you, the members of the Press, the people of South Sudan and the International community, that I am not afraid of the Court, and will welcome a full and thorough investigation, conducted with full transparency, that will disclose the full facts and truth behind the discrepancies and missing funds, and I can assure you that the true corrupt individuals will be exposed by a proper investigation of the facts. This Nation must stand proud. We fought a war and won it. We had our referendum and won it 98% and won our independence.

We must now fight and win our financial war, both here at home and with Khartoum.

Thank you very much.
Hon. Arthur Akuien Chol

After the press conference, Pagan Amum, SPLM's Secretary-General, sued me for defamation for accusing him of receiving US$30,000,000 in 2006. Several weeks later, the court acquitted Amum based on insufficient evidence. I appealed this decision because I have all the evidence to corroborate my accusations. But 10 years later, no judgement has been handed down. It is deeply distressing to live with this uncertainty.

CHAPTER 18

ACHIEVING INDEPENDENCE

Tragically, the Comprehensive Peace Agreement's 'permanent' cease fire was short-lived and in November 2006, hundreds of our people died in brutal fighting between the Sudanese army and former rebels in the Upper Nile State's capital, Malakal. It was the heaviest fighting since the civil war ended in 2005. Eighteen months later, disagreements about the disputed oil-rich Abyei area on the border between South Sudan and the north escalated, resulting in clashes between the SPLA and an Arab militia. The following year, an arbitration court in The Hague shrank the disputed Abyei region and placed the major Heglig oil field in the north. Reluctantly, the South Sudan accepted the court's ruling, but unfortunately, conflict continued.

One major impediment to the cohesive and effective development of South Sudan is what we call tribalism. It had its genesis in the war with the government of Sudan. Using the age-old tactic of divide-and-rule, Khartoum pitted one tribe against the other. It had the desired effect of one ethnic group fighting against the other. The Sudan government played favourite with one tribe by supplying them with arms and building development projects in their homeland while neglecting the other tribe. This unhealthy state of affairs continued until South Sudan seceded from the north. Until then, 'tribal wars' were all over the place, which led to insecurity and the death and displacement of millions of our people.

The Government of Sudan was also skilled at nepotism, which was highly encouraged in the government's employment system. Many prominent government officials employed their relatives in vital government positions, but no-one gave a hoot about whether a person employed in a position was the most suitable candidate. Such a corrupt system of hiring staff resulted in an inefficient and unprofessional public service. Needless to say, productivity was almost zero.

Meanwhile, as stipulated by the Comprehensive Peace Agreement, a referendum on secession occurred in January 2011. After two decades of guerrilla warfare that claimed the lives of over 1.5 million people and displaced four million or more, our people voted in favour of full independence from the north. It was an extraordinary achievement for South Sudan, although bitter-sweet because of the unimaginable suffering that preceded it. Unfortunately, independence did not bring conflict to an end.

While President Omar al-Bashir acknowledged the South's secession, tensions remained high because of several unresolved issues, particularly the unequal sharing of oil revenues. Four months after the referendum, Bashir's forces occupied the Abyei region, but in June 2011, the north and South signed an accord to demilitarise the Abyei region and allow Ethiopian peacekeeping forces to enter. Unfortunately, that did not put an end to the conflict.

Memories of 9 July 2011, South Sudan's Independence Day, will be etched in my heart forever. It is the day the world's newest nation, South Sudan, was born and *Salva Kiir* Mayardit became its first President. Like most of our people, I was euphoric and hoped for a peaceful future for South Sudan. My great hope was that South Sudan's oil revenues would be invested in building schools, hospitals, roads and providing electricity and drinking water to urban and rural communities. I longed for my nation to give our children and young people the opportunity of a quality education. Devastatingly, those hopes were dashed when fighting resumed, not with the north but between South Sudan's ethnic groups.

The principal source of conflict was rivalry between President Kiir and the Vice-President Dr Riek Macher. Kiir suspected Macher of plotting to unseat him as President, but rather than remaining a power struggle between two men, it engulfed the ethnic groups they represented. Like John Garang, Salva Kiir is a Dinka, the largest ethnic group in the south, whereas Riak Macher is a Neur, the second-largest ethnic grouping; disputes between them reflected ethnic, regional and political rivalries extending back to the second civil war that escalated after John Garang's death. Despite Machar's return to the SPLM after his defection, many Dinka did not trust him, heightening hostilities between the Dinka and Neur people.

One month after achieving independence, our hopes for a peaceful Sudan were shattered when ethnic clashes broke out in Jonglei state. By August 2011, the United Nations reported the deaths of at least 600 people and 100,000 had fled to refugee camps in neighbouring countries. In January 2012, South Sudan declared a state of disaster in the region.

Three months later, after weeks of border fighting—the Heglig Crisis—southern forces occupied the oil-rich border town of Heglig. It did not take long for the Sudanese army to force the rebels out, but in the meantime, 200,000 refugees had fled into South Sudan to escape the violence. In June 2012, a peace deal that created a 10-kilometre demilitarised zone along the border was reached, enabling South Sudan's oil exports to resume, and in September 2012 after several days of peace talks in Ethiopia, Bashir and Kiir signed trade, oil and security agreements.

But that was not the end of conflict and on 15 December 2013, civil war broke out in South Sudan after President Kiir sacked the nation's cabinet and accused Machar of plotting a failed coup. Conflict soared during the next few days, quickly drawing in Jonglei, Unity and Upper Nile. Rebel factions seized control of several regional towns, killing thousands and displacing over 2.2 million people. Between January 2014 and 2018, Kiir and Macher signed several peace deals to end South Sudan's civil war, but they breached each of them and fighting continued between the Dinka and Neur. Finally, in August 2018, Kiir signed a power sharing agreement with Machar and other opposition groups that ended South Sudan's civil war. This resulted in a fragile peace, although hostilities continued, with fighting between the government and opposition and within rebel factions in parts of Unity, Upper Nile and Central Equatoria.

Meanwhile, the impact of decades of brutal war, severe droughts in 2011 and 2015, devastating floods in 2014, 2017, 2019, 2020, 2021 and 2022, and COVID-19 have resulted in a humanitarian crisis in South Sudan. Most of my people need humanitarian assistance, especially women and children. My nation must implement its peace agreement to bring an end to the conflict that has ravaged it for decade after decade. It must also build vital infrastructure, strengthen governance, educate our children and young people, use its oil revenues to fund sustainable economic development rather than war, and build resilience against future catastrophic weather events.

CHAPTER 19

SEEKING REFUGE IN AUSTRALIA

In 1998, Australia granted asylum to Teresa, and six of our children. Mary and two of our children, Angok and Deng, lived in Kenya with me while completing their education. Lual was also in Kenya with me when his mother Teresa and the rest of his siblings were granted asylum in Australia. Teresa had started the process in 1995, so she endured a lengthy, soul-destroying wait. She'd queue for hours in the scorching sun, even resorting to sleeping in the street, to gain an interview with United Nations and Embassy officials. After Canada and America rejected her applications, Teresa applied to the Australian Embassy. To our immense relief, Australia accepted our family.

At first, Teresa and our children lived in community housing in Doonside, then they rented a house in Ashfield. Later, they moved to South Strathfield, then Croydon Park. In 2003, National Australia Bank approved a mortgage application for us to borrow the funds to purchase a house in Minchinbury, our family home. All our children live in surrounding suburbs, which is wonderful.

In 2000, Australia accepted Lual as a refugee, but he too endured a lengthy process to get here. However, to his great surprise, two weeks after arriving, he took part in the opening ceremony of Sydney's Olympic Games; he waved from a truck with other South Sudanese as it circled around the main arena. It was a glorious welcome to his new home. Lual returned to South Sudan in 2011 to run the construction company he owned, coming back here five years later. I remained as South Sudan's Minister of Finance, then a member of its Council of States and came to Australia on 11 September 2001, the day the World Trade Centre towers fell in New York. Angok was my private secretary for several years and he joined his siblings in 2003. Teresa, our children and I are now proud Australia citizens.

In 2016, Angok was nominated to South Sudan's Parliament and like me, he travelled to South Sudan for Parliamentary sittings, returning home to our family during holidays. He took time off from politics in 2021 because serving his country meant he had to spend too much time away from his wife and children in Australia.

When I first came to Australia and spoke with my children about their education, I was amazed about Australia's higher education system and how the government pays students' university fees, which young people pay back after they graduate and start working. Immediately, I thought that if South Sudan had implemented this system when I was young, my country would be in a much better position now. I went through hell to get educated, but I was one of the few lucky ones, for which I am immensely grateful. But it should not have been so difficult, and South Sudanese students should not have to rely on scholarships and the generosity of donors; access to educational opportunities should be available to everyone. Still, my education served me well, enabling me to reach what I call the epitome of service to my nation. Education gave me the opportunity to build South

Sudan's economic foundations and serve as a vital figure among the first generation of our nation's leaders.

Soon I will retire as the representative of my people on the Council of States and spend more time in Australia, my new home. I cannot help but compare the two nations I call home. Modern Australia is just over 200 years old, and I keep asking myself if it will be possible for South Sudan to progress to Australia's current level of development in the next 200 years? I dearly hope so, but first it must overcome ethnic, regional and political divides and focus on building a sustainable future for my people.

EPILOGUE

As one of South Sudan's first generation of political leaders, one who has devoted his life to improving the quality of life of my people, I am reflecting on why South Sudan is suffering a dire humanitarian crisis despite its great wealth as an oil exporter. The principal reason is that it has squandered millions of dollars of oil revenues funding war, first with the north, and now among its different ethnic groups within South Sudan itself. Another major factor is that it has not invested in the vital infrastructure it requires for economic and social development.

When I was Minister for Finance, I funded a network

of roads throughout South Sudan and between the north and South, but many of these roads and bridges were destroyed during the South's civil war. I believe the government must prioritise the construction of asphalted roads because roads are required to connect production centres of goods and food to population centres and rural areas.

In 1974 when I was first elected to Parliament, I also arranged for the railway line to be refurbished in Aweil and proposed for a new line that would link Aweil to the rest of South Sudan, but this proposal never took shape because of the war. It is the same story for the rest of South Sudan's rail network. The government must give railway construction serious consideration because it is less costly and more efficient at linking all regions of the country than constructing a nationwide roads network. River transport, bridges over rivers, land and air cargo, would all help improve the country's flow of goods from places of production to areas of consumption.

Other major tasks include eradicating tribalism, conflict within the SPLM, systemic corruption and the entrenched nepotism that means unqualified people are appointed to senior positions. This is why providing quality education and technical training is crucial for my country to ensure qualified professionals are appointed to key positions rather than friends and family of those in power.

My dream is that South Sudan will recover from decades of war, build resistance to climate change and the catastrophic floods and droughts it causes, invest in infrastructure and education, eradicate systemic violence and human rights abuses, and address its devastating humanitarian crisis.

During the last five decades, I have done my best to achieve Garang's vision, but we need a new generation of educated South Sudanese to run our country, young people who are honest and dedicate themselves to developing our nation. That is what it will take for my country to build a sustainable economy and promote John Garang's vision of democracy, social justice, equality, political stability and peace.

I have always encouraged my children to study, and I am pleased they have respected my wishes to gain a sound education. I feel blessed that my children are proud of me and see me as their role model, but I wish that blessing for all parents and grandparents. South Sudan should educate its young people itself but until it does so, the only option is for my children and South Sudanese refugees living in Australia and other nations to embrace education then return to South Sudan as its next generation of political leaders and qualified professionals.

I love Australia. It is a wealthy country, and most people have a job. Here, there is respect for the law. My children are peaceful because they live in a harmonious society. They have a lot of friends, and they are learning many things. Australia is a country that gives them the opportunity to grow and secure a better future for themselves and their children. This is my wish for South Sudan—for my country to be peaceful and to give opportunities to the younger generation to learn, grow and provide for their future needs and those of their families.

ACKNOWLEDGEMENTS

I owe my heartfelt thanks to my father, the late Chol Dut Akol, for opening up the world of education to me rather than insisting I remain a cattle boy on the swampy grasslands of Aweil South in South Sudan. Waa also inspired me to serve my country and people as a political leader. The course of my life would have been profoundly different without Waa's early guidance and support.

The late William Deng Nhial, Dr John Garang de Mabior and President Salva Kiir Mayardit also shaped my life, and I appreciate the opportunities and counsel they offered me. They trusted me to serve our people and nation, an honour for which I am immensely grateful.

Teresa Awien Mawien Diing and Mary Adut Achor Dhel, my wives, have played a crucial role in my life too, and I owe them my deepest gratitude. They gave me the greatest gift, nine beautiful children, and helped me raise each of them to be kind, honest, empathetic and loving. Like me, Teresa and Mary encouraged our children to pursue an education, one of my greatest wishes for all children. They also kept our family together at the most challenging times of our lives, ensuring we remain close even when living in different countries.

For over four decades, Teresa and Mary's love and support enabled me to serve my people as a founding political leader of South Sudan. Without their commitment and sacrifices, I would not have been able to pursue such a demanding political career or enjoy the blessing of being surrounded by my beautiful family.

My family means everything to me, and I am immensely proud of each of my children. I am deeply grateful for the unconditional love of my daughters, Awut Arthur Akuien Chol and Achol Arthur Akuien Chol, and for that of my sons: Deng Arthur Akuien Chol; Akot Arthur Akuien; Deng Arthur Akuien Jnr; Angok Arthur Akuien Jnr and Chol Arthur Akuien.

I am also grateful my children's partners have become significant pillars of my family. I wish to thank my son-in-law, George Uliny Kang, and daughters-in-law, Awien Cleto Akot Kuel, Anguec Lewis Dut Uguak and Veronica Apuk Deng Chier.

My sons Lual Arthur Akuien Chol and Angok Arthur Akuien Chol took considerable time out of their busy family schedules to help me produce my biography, for which I am immensely grateful. Also my thanks to Gabriella and African World Book Press's Peter Deng.

And I want to acknowledge the resilience and patriotism of the people of South Sudan for enduring decades of struggle to achieve independence for our nation. It is thanks to you that South Sudan is now an independent nation.

The University of Freiburg, Freiburg Switzerland as a student in 1967.

In Switzerland with a colleague during the time of my studies in 1967.

University of Freiburg, posing with a colleague in front of the library entrance, 1967.

*At the University compound,
Freiburg Switzerland in 1967.*

In Juba with colleagues from the Commission for Resettlement in mid 1970s.

With Albino Akol Akol in Aweil, 1970s.

With my colleagues during my studies at Univerité Lovanium in Kinshasa Congo in early 1960s.

With my wife Teresa Awien and Son Lual Arthur Akuien in 1978.

A LIFE FIGHTING FOR MY PEOPLE

With Martin Majier, William Ajal Deng Gai, and other colleagues in mid 1970s.

With the late Dr. John Garang de Mabior, late Lual Diing Wol, Malong Awan, and Chuor Deng Mareng, Nairobi Kenya, in 2001.

With Teresa Awien Mawien Diing, our daughters Awut Arthur Akuien Chol, Achol Arthur Akuien Chol, and sons Lual, Deng, Akot, Angok Jnr and Chol Arthur Akuien Chol, Alexandria Egypt in 1995.

In Congo with fellow university colleagues in early 1960s.

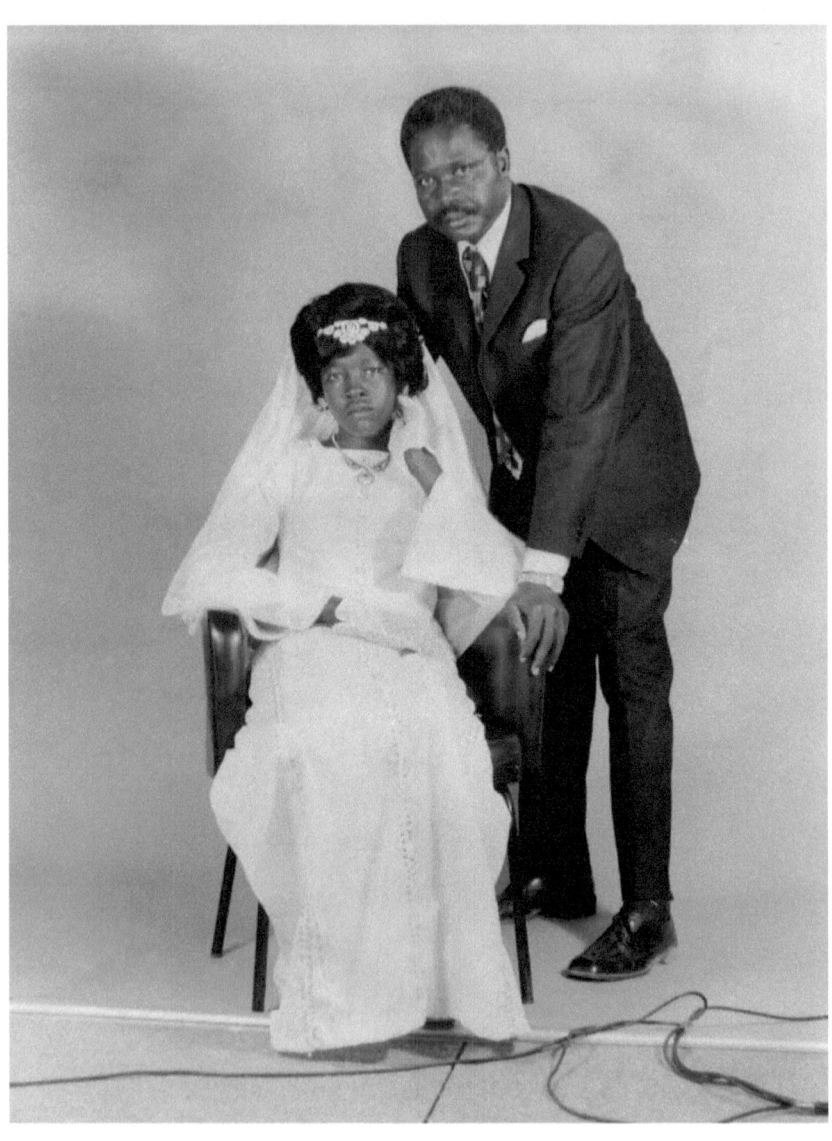

During my wedding day to TeresaAwien Mawien Diing in Aweil, South Sudan 1975.

*My wife Teresa Awien Mawien Diing
in Alexandria Egypt, 1996.*

With my wife Teresa Awien Mawien Diing in Alexandria Egypt, 1996.

*With my wife Mary Adut Achor Dhel
in Alexandria Egypt, 1990.*

ARTHUR AKUIEN CHOL

With my wife Mary Adut Achor Dhel, and sons Deng Arthur Akuien Chol Jnr and Angok Arthur Akuien Chol in Alexandria Egypt, 1990.

My wife Mary Adut Achor Dhel in Alexandria Egypt, 1990.

With my children, Achol Arthur Akuien Chol and Chol Arthur Akuien Chol, Alexandria Egypt, 1996.

My wife Teresa Awien and son Chol Arthur Akuien Chol, Sydney, Australia, 2020.

My father Chol Dut Akol with my wives Teresa and Mary and my son Deng Arthur Akuien in Khartoum in the early 80s.

My son Angok Arthur Akuien, Northern Bahr el Ghazal State-Awiel, South Sudan, during a public rally in 2020.

My son Angok Arthur Akuien Jnr, Juba, 2021.

*My son Akot Arthur Akuien
at a work-related conference, 2022.*

My daughter Awut Arthur Akuien with her family in Sydney Australia, 2019.

My son Deng Arthur Akuien Chol with his family in NSW Australia, 2019.

My son Lual Arthur Akuien with his family in Sydney Australia, 2022.

With my son Angok Arthur Akuien and his family during my grandson's primary school graduation in Sydney Australia, 2022.

My son Lual Arthur Akuien during his graduation in 2010 in Sydney Australia.

My son Angok Arthur Akuien Chol during his graduation in 2008.

With my son Lual Arthur Akuien and foreign investors, Juba South Sudan, 2011.

*My sons Lual and Angok Arthur Akuien Chol,
Juba, South Sudan, 2013.*

*My wives Teresa and Mary with relatives
in Alexandria Egypt, 1992.*

My daughter In-Law, Apuk Deng Chier during her union with my son Akot Arthur Akuien in Adelaide Australia, 2017.

During my press release in Juba, South Sudan, 2012.

My wife Teresa with our grandchildren, Sydney Australia, 2018.

With my wife Teresa Awien in Sydney Australia, 2023.

*My wife Teresa and our grandchildren,
Abuk Chol Arthur Akuien and Chol Deng Arthur Akuien,
in Sydney, Australia, in 2023.*

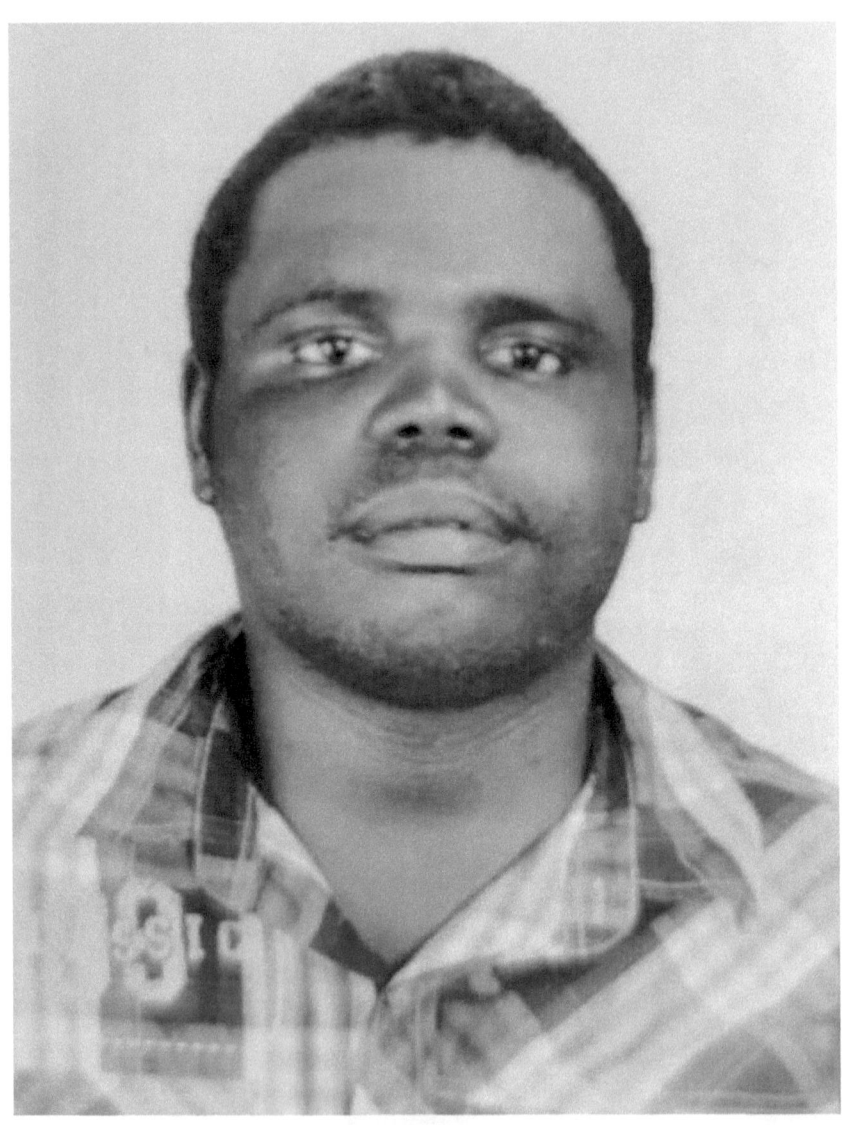

*My son Deng Arthur Akuien
in Juba, South Sudan, in 2022.*

*My youngest daughter, Achol Arthur Akuien,
Sydney, Australia, 2023.*

With my grandson Angok Angok Arthur Akuien in Nairobi, Kenya, in 2021.

With the youngest of my grandchildren during my recent visit to Sydney, Australia, in 2023.

*My Son Akot Arthur Akuien Chol
and his family in Nairobi Kenya, 2023.*

*My son Akot Arthur Akuien
during his graduation in Brisbane Australia, 2009.*

www.ingramcontent.com/pod-product-compliance
Lightning Source LLC
Chambersburg PA
CBHW030256010526
44107CB00053B/1736